Ella Fitzgerald

AVAILABLE UP CLOSE TITLES:

RACHEL CARSON by Ellen Levine

JOHNNY CASH by Anne E. Neimark

ELLA FITZGERALD by Tanya Lee Stone

ROBERT F. KENNEDY by Marc Aronson

ELVIS PRESLEY by Wilborn Hampton

JOHN STEINBECK by Milton Meltzer

OPRAH WINFREY by Ilene Cooper

FRANK LLOYD WRIGHT by Jan Adkins

FUTURE UP CLOSE TITLES:

W. E. B. DU BOIS by Tonya Bolden

BILL GATES by Marc Aronson

JANE GOODALL by Sudipta Bardhan-Quallen

HARPER LEE by Kerry Madden

THURGOOD MARSHALL by Chris Crowe

BABE RUTH by Wilborn Hampton

UP_close:_

Ella Fitzgerald

a twentieth-century life by
TANYA LEE STONE

VIKING

VIKING

Published by Penguin Group

Penguin Young Readers Group, 345 Hudson Street, New York, New York 10014, U.S.A.

Penguin Group (Canada), 90 Eglinton Avenue East, Suite 700, Toronto, Ontario,

Canada M4P 2Y3 (a division of Pearson Penguin Canada Inc.)

Penguin Books Ltd, 80 Strand, London WC2R 0RL, England

Penguin Ireland, 25 St Stephen's Green, Dublin 2, Ireland (a division of Penguin Books Ltd)

Penguin Group (Australia), 250 Camberwell Road, Camberwell, Victoria 3124, Australia

(a division of Pearson Australia Group Pty Ltd)

Penguin Books India Pvt Ltd, 11 Community Centre, Panchsheel Park, New Delhi – 110 017, India

Penguin Group (NZ), 67 Apollo Drive, Rosedale, North Shore 0632, New Zealand

(a division of Pearson New Zealand Ltd)

Penguin Books (South Africa) (Pty) Ltd, 24 Sturdee Avenue, Rosebank, Johannesburg 2196,

South Africa

Penguin Books Ltd, Registered Offices: 80 Strand, London WC2R 0RL, England

First published in 2008 by Viking, a division of Penguin Young Readers Group

10 9 8 7 6 5 4 3 2

LIBRARY OF CONGRESS CATALOGING-IN-PUBLICATION DATA

Stone, Tanya Lee.

Up close, Ella Fitzgerald / By Tanya Lee Stone.

p. cm. — (Up close)

ISBN 978-0-670-06149-5 (hardcover)

1. Fitzgerald, Ella—Juvenile literature. 2. Singers—United States—Biography—Juvenile literature.

I. Title.

ML3930.F5S76 2008

782.42165092—dc22

[B] 2007023117

Printed in the U.S.A.

Set in Goudy

Book design by Jim Hoover

For Sarah and Leah, with love.
May all of your dreams come true.

Contents

Ella Fitzgerald

Author's Note

ELLA FITZGERALD WAS a megastar, but she kept her private life incredibly close. There has always been a mystique surrounding this legend. She was a private soul, protective of the details that made up her life. This fact led to major challenges in researching her story. Thankfully, sorting it all out was made infinitely less daunting by historian and jazz expert Stuart Nicholson's essential book for adults, *Ella Fitzgerald: The Complete Biography*. Most previous accounts of Ella's life were muddied by misinformation, exaggerations, and half-truths, many of which were intended to clean up what was a somewhat messy start to life. But the Nicholson biography sets the record straight on many anecdotes of Ella's history. I would like to thank Mr. Nicholson, both for writing an excellent account of Ella's life, and for offering feedback on this book.

Foreword

I GREW UP NEAR New Haven, Connecticut, a city close enough to New York City to be a stop on many a musician's tour schedule. New Haven was, and still is, a hot spot for all kinds of music. Yale University's Woolsey Hall hosted the best of the best in the music world, and my father made sure we were exposed to a lot of it. From the time I was so young my legs dangled from the seats, I visited Woolsey Hall and heard both the Yale and New Haven Symphony orchestras multiple times, and was lucky enough to be introduced to a variety of music that included the lyrical classical guitar of Andrés Segovia, the exuberant marching-band music of John Philip Sousa, and the red-hot jazz of Dizzy Gillespie. I'll never forget the sheer fun of seeing Dizzy's trademark move in action—he puffed his cheeks out huge and round as he wailed on his trumpet!

New Haven is also home to a world-class jazz festival. I used to go to the festival with my friends from the performing arts high school where I was a music major studying voice. We soaked up everything we could about music history and theory, we played in ensembles—jazz and classical, vocal and instrumental— and bounded off to the jazz festival together to take in the sights and sounds of the hippest folks in the industry. It was a trip! I still have the now-faded posters from those jazz festivals. They hung on my walls in high school and traveled with me for dorm-room decorations at Oberlin College—where I studied voice at the Conservatory of Music. I didn't realize the full impact of just how fortunate I was to have grown up in New Haven to hear those greats live and in person until much later, reading the many names off those old posters that cataloged a veritable Who's Who of jazz.

Even though I trained as a classical vocalist, I was way into Billie Holiday, Sarah Vaughan—and of course, Ella Fitzgerald. Theirs were the songs I gravitated toward when given the chance to sidle up to a piano bar. There is no doubt that my comrades' taste in music influenced me. There's nothing like a wild-eyed guy all hopped up on Sonny Rollins and Artie Shaw to make a girl sit up and take notice.

Jay Rowe, a jazz-piano student at the time—and now a great pianist—had an infectious passion for all that was jazz. He couldn't wait to play me a Dave Brubeck album or marvel at the fact that I hadn't ever heard Charlie Parker (a.k.a., the Bird) blow. I haven't seen Jay for more than twenty-five years, but if I close my eyes I can still see the smile that took over his entire face when he listened to, or even talked about, jazz. Man, it was infectious! It had me wanting to say "cat" and "gig."

And I'll never forget hearing Ella sing for the first time. On went the record and out came this voice that sounded like butterscotch. It permeated the room, mesmerizing me with its soothing tone. From then on, anytime I wanted to change my mood and feel calm or peaceful, an Ella album would be one of the first things I would reach for. All of these memories flooded over me as I started to research Ella Fitzgerald's life and treat my ears to her smooth, velvety tone. I am proud to be able to contribute to the body of literature about this American icon of jazz.

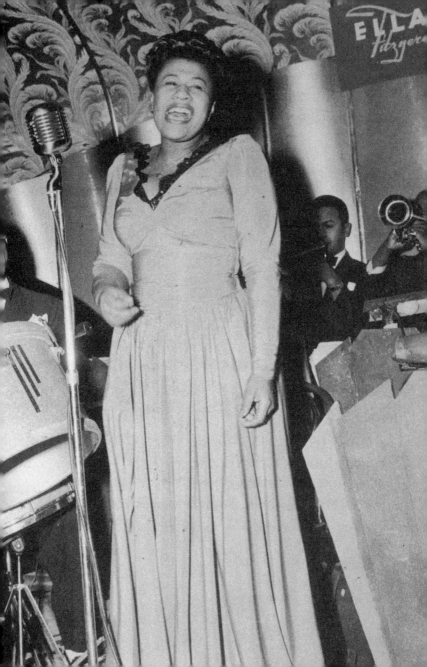

Introduction

ON JUNE 12, 1935, Ella Fitzgerald walked into the Decca recording studios. Just a little more than six months earlier, a teenage Ella was living on the streets of New York, scraping to get by. She struggled just to have enough to eat and a clean place to sleep. But by summer, everything had changed. She was singing with a band. A big band. A successful band.

It must have been exciting—and probably a bit overwhelming, too. One minute she was homeless. The next, she was poised to be a star. Her voice, smooth as silk, pure as honey, had given her a new home with the Chick Webb Band. Ella was ready to make her first record. The song was "Love and Kisses," and with lively horns accompanying her, Ella's young

Ella performs at the Savoy Ballroom in New York City, 1941.

voice carried the song with an innocence that made it instantly appealing.

Love and kisses, never misses,
making a heaven for two.
With the tender, sweet surrender,
coming from someone like you.

When the record was released, Ella was on tour with the Chick Webb Band. The group was in Philadelphia and she was itching to hear her song. There was a jukebox at a nearby bar, but she was too young to be let in to a place that served alcohol. Determined to hear it, Ella had someone else go in and put money in the jukebox for her. Then she stood outside the door, listening. Hearing her own voice on a record for the first time must have been profound. Ella couldn't have known that that first cut was just the beginning of a long, illustrious recording career.

Hear what some of her colleagues, friends, and admirers had to say about Ella Fitzgerald.

Producer Quincy Jones: "When you listen to Ella, you hear a jazz musician interpreting the melody, blending variations of phrasing, melody, rhythm and spontaneous improvisation. She could use her exquisite, very human voice just like a saxophone, sometimes like a violin, sometimes like a trumpet."

Singer Mel Tormé: "Male or female, she was it. She was the best singer on the planet."

Singer Johnny Mathis: "She was the best there ever was. Amongst all of us who sing. She was the best."

Pianist Lou Levy: "Ella was divine. You can't get better than that. It will never be that good again."

Entertainer Bing Crosby: "Man, woman and child, Ella Fitzgerald is the greatest!"

COTTON CLUB
The WORLD FAMOUS
COTTON CLUB
BILL ROBINSON
COTTON CLUB PARADE
DINNER $1.50
COTTON CLUB
ANN LEWIS
WHYTE MANIACS
BEAUTY SALON
SANDWICHES
MANICURE 35¢

One

"We were all poor in that neighborhood then."

IN NEWPORT NEWS, Virginia, Temperance (Tempie) Fitzgerald gave birth to a baby girl. Contrary to what many history books report, however, the date was April 25, 1917—not 1918. And so began the life of Ella Fitzgerald—a life lived largely in the public eye but whose private details were well guarded.

Tempie and William Fitzgerald, Ella's biological father, lived together in Virginia but never married. Although William gave them both his last name, he had left by the time Ella was three years old. Tempie had been working as a laundress when she met Joseph Da Silva and he became the new man in her life.

Things were difficult for African American

The Cotton Club in 1932. One of the hottest spots in Harlem.

communities in the South. Racism was rampant, and the South was segregated under the Jim Crow laws. These laws stated that African Americans were "separate but equal," which, in reality, translated into separate and inferior. African Americans went to separate schools, had separate drinking fountains, and used separate entrances to public buildings. The attitude toward African Americans in the South was much more negative than in the North.

In addition, economic conditions in the South were poor, especially for African Americans. Stories of better jobs and more racial tolerance in Northern cities triggered a massive move between 1910 and 1930, in what became known as the Great Migration. Many Northern jobs were created with the boom in production during World War I. Some Southern employers tried to convince their workers to stay, with promises of improving conditions and pay. Others took a different approach, boarding northbound trains and using force to try and make African American workers get off and stay in their current jobs.

Still, the Great Migration continued. In fact, an estimated one million African Americans left the

South and headed for the North. Tempie, Joe, and Ella were among them. They took a chance at a better life and left Virginia. Along with Chicago, Cleveland, and Detroit, New York City was one of the cities that saw the largest population increase, and that's exactly where they went.

Unfortunately, the Great Migration was filled with disappointment for many. The number of available jobs could not keep up with the steady incoming flow of people, who often ended up swapping one bad set of circumstances for another. This was true for Ella's family. Although they found shelter at 27 Clinton Street in Yonkers, New York, it was in just one room for all three of them. Joe took odd jobs and Tempie once again got work as a laundress, this time at the Silver Lining Laundry. But even with a roof over their heads and some money coming in, things were tight.

In 1923, Tempie had another daughter. She and Joe named her Frances, and gave Ella's half-sister Joe's last name, Da Silva. In September of that same year, six-year-old Ella started at Public School 10 in Yonkers, just down the street from where they lived. In the summer of 1925, Ella's family moved five blocks away, to a large apartment building at 72 School Street. Their neighborhood was made up largely of Italians and blacks, with smaller numbers of Irish, Greek, and other ethnic groups. A girl Ella knew as a kid, Josephine Attanasio, remembered, "We were *all* poor in that neighborhood then. . . . Where I lived was mostly Italian, and where Ella lived was with the black kids down below. . . . It was a little rough."

In fact, one of the "rough" moments Ella experienced was *with* Attanasio, during the fourth grade. Apparently, Ella said something to Josephine's little sister that scared the girl. Josephine got into a tussle with Ella over it, and Ella bloodied her nose. This story later turned into an incorrect tale about Ella beating up a boy who had insulted her. But Attanasio set the record straight. "We had a little fight and she [Ella] gave me a bloody nose. She intimidated my younger sister. . . . I ran down and had it out with her!"

But besides the odd clash now and then, people who lived in that neighborhood at the time recall an atmosphere in which different ethnic groups got along fairly well. One childhood friend of Ella's, a middle-class Italian girl named Rose Sarubbi, talked about their growing up together. "Ella would always come to our home and loved eating my mother's spaghetti," she remembered.

Rose's impression of Ella was that of "a very happy girl who loved to dance and sing." There didn't seem to be much musical influence at home or at school, though, except for some piano lessons her mother may have arranged when she could scrounge the extra pennies. Ella did say, "My mother had a very beautiful, classical voice. . . . But I don't think she ever really did too much of it. They tell me that my father was a guitar player, but I don't know." Ella had some opportunity to sing as a result of attending church. She went to services and Sunday school at the Bethany African Methodist Episcopal Church in Yonkers. She may have also sung at other local churches, as another childhood friend, Annette Gulliver, remembered that it was common for kids to go to their friends' churches, as well. The church inspires future singers all the time. It's easy for a person with a heart for music to pick up rhythm, tone, and style from the resounding sound of a church filled with music.

Radio had a big influence on Ella, too. When she was young, it was relatively new that radio was available to the general public. Ella had a natural talent for imitating singers and song styles. She liked to teach her friends the newest hits, such as "Sweet Thing" and "Fidgety Feet." Her ability to sing helped make her popular with both girls and boys, even though the boys didn't seem to find her attractive. But Ella's joy was infectious, and it made people like her. She seemed to lighten the overall mood of her neighborhood. Attanasio remembered, "She just smiled all the time, just shaking her shoulders and singing. She had dangling earrings, those big hoops, and broken-down shoes."

Even more than singing, though, Ella was passionate about dancing. She and Annette's brother Charles were thick as thieves, starting in the third grade. They would hang around outside the school or in the streets and just dance and dance. They liked to learn new dances from the older kids, then turn around and teach the steps to their friends. Annette remembered, "She would get up and sing and dance—her, my brother, and my nephew would dance, the three of them. It was then that we'd say Ella was going to go places, as a dancer!"

As Ella and Charles got a bit older, they took their dancing even more seriously. Living in Yonkers, they were not far from the dancehalls and jazz clubs of Harlem, New York City. In the late 1920s, that was where the pulse of jazz was beating. In fact, Harlem was experiencing what would later be called the Harlem Renaissance—a period of time when African American artists, writers, and musicians were flourishing. In part, the Harlem Renaissance resulted from the Great Migration, which brought so many African Americans to New York City. Norma Miller, a dancer, remembered: "When the bands got up on those bandstands and played music, well naturally, the music emanated out of the ballroom into the street. So you could always hear music on the streets of Harlem." The huge Savoy Ballroom, which took up a whole block on Lenox Avenue from 140th to 141st Street, and the Cotton Club on 142nd Street were among the hottest spots of all. The Savoy had opened in 1926, built from the ground up where once there had been just a vacant lot. Charles and Ella would take a trolley and then a subway from Yonkers into Harlem and slip into the dance clubs. Many of the clubs had amateur nights where a dancer could perform and compete, sometimes for prize money. Charles and Ella also found sporadic work dancing at the clubs in Yonkers.

Charles said about Ella, "She was some dancer, oh yeah! . . . We used to go down to . . . the Savoy. We'd learn all the latest dances." At that time, dances like the Shimmy and the Lindy Hop were all the rage. Ella particularly loved the moves of a dancer named Snake Hips Tucker. "Snake Hips Tucker. She used to like that. She was crazy about that type of dancing," Charles said. And in an interview in her later years with conductor André Previn, Ella recalled, "There was a man called Snake Hips. And I used to try to dance. . . . Snake Hips Fitzgerald," she teased Previn with a wry smile.

Ella was young and full of spunk. But when her mother died in 1932, things changed. There are two stories about her mother's death, and it's difficult to know which one is true. At one point, Ella gave a story to the press that told of her mother holding a young boy on her lap in the front passenger seat of a car. When the driver stopped short, Tempie moved to protect him and hit her head in the process. According to Ella, the wound never healed. However, Annette and Charles Gulliver were not aware of this event, which seems unlikely, given how dramatic it would have been and how close Ella was to the Gulliver siblings. The other story that was reported was that Tempie died as the result of a heart attack. Regardless of which account is accurate, Ella's life took a turn for the worse upon her mother's death.

Joe Da Silva did not take kindly to his fifteen-year-old stepdaughter's habit of staying out late dancing. When Ella and Charles got back one night, Da Silva punished her by confining her to the house. "He made her stay in the house for quite a while," Charles said. There is some evidence that Da Silva began drinking, and word began to carry through the neighborhood that all was not right at home between Ella and Da Silva. Charles later said, "I sensed that he wasn't kind to her. You could sense what was going on, y'know, from her actions. But I would never ask her . . . did he mistreat you . . . because she wouldn't tell me anyway."

Whatever was going on, it was enough to prompt Tempie's sister, Ella's aunt Virginia, to remove Ella from the household. Virginia lived in Harlem, and Ella moved in with her and her cousin Georgiana at West 145th Street. She left the high school she had been attending in Yonkers, and Charles and Annette did not see much of her from then on. Not long after, Da Silva died from a heart attack, and Ella's half-sister Frances also moved in with their aunt Virginia.

Although Ella loved Frances very much, she was in dire need of attention, and sharing Virginia with both Frances and Georgiana was likely hard on her. Money was also tight. Ella dropped out of school and started getting into some trouble, taking to the streets to find ways to drum up some cash. There was an illegal lottery being run in Harlem at the time, and Ella got involved with the scheme. (The lottery we are familiar with today is a legal form of gambling, but this lottery was not regulated and was against the law.) June Norton, a woman close to Ella in later years, said,

"She [Ella] probably was running numbers for people who were just using kids . . . and she's just delivering something and . . . didn't realize, that that was, I think, illegal. And if she did, y'know, she had to live."

Because she was absent from school and getting into trouble on the streets, the police eventually got involved, and a family court ruled in 1934 that Ella should be put in a home for girls. She was sent to the New York State Training School for Girls in upstate New York, near Albany. Most of the girls were only sent there for minor issues, such as being absent from school repeatedly, yet it was later discovered that they were treated horribly. *New York Times* journalist Nina Bernstein reported, "She ended up in this place up the Hudson River with a very harsh and really punitive regime. These girls were routinely beaten by male staff."

In 1965, the then-famous Ella was invited to return and speak to the girls living there at the time, but she refused. She never wanted to set foot in that place again and, in fact, never talked about the experience in public. Historians and reporters, in the course of doing research about her life, pieced together the story. In 1996, Bernstein interviewed a former superintendent of the home who said about Ella, "She hated the place. She had been held in the basement of one of the cottages once and all but tortured. She was [not] . . . going to come back."

In the fall of 1934, Ella managed to run away from the home. She couldn't go back to her aunt's house, because she would have been picked up by the police for escaping and promptly shipped back. Since she still dreamed of being a performer, Ella struck out for the city even though the Great Depression was in full swing.

It had begun with the stock market crash in 1929 and lasted through the early 1930s. Banks failed, businesses went bankrupt, and people were out of work all over. A domino effect was triggered by a lack of economic activity. As jobs continued to disappear, cities were hit harder and harder, and Harlem was no exception. The euphoria of the Harlem Renaissance had died down a bit, becoming overshadowed by the enormous economic hardships as black unemployment rates soared. Money was scarce. Ella certainly had none.

June Norton said, "She never cried in her beer about circumstances because it wasn't going to make things different. It wasn't going to change what was. And so the best she could do was to pick up from there, and go on." Ella did just that. She picked herself up, dusted herself off, and headed to Harlem to try and make it as a dancer.

HARLEM OPERA HOUSE

Greatest SHOW VALUE in Harlem

125th ST. west of 7th Ave. *Phone* UN-4-8519

ONE WEEK — BEGINNING FRIDAY, FEBRUARY 15TH

Tiny Bradshaw

And His Sensational BAND

MAE ALIX—EDDIE HUNTER—BILLY HIGGINS
3 SAMS—GEORGE BOOKER—ELLA FITZGERALD

Special Added Attraction
MAE WHITMAN Presents

POPS AND LOUIE
WITH **ALICE WHITMAN**
in a wonderful new act

On the Screen **"MENACE"** Mystery Melodrama | First Chapter "Rustlers of Red Dog"

ONE WEEK ONLY — BEGINNING FRIDAY, FEB. 22ND

GREATEST EVENT IN THEATRICAL HISTORY!

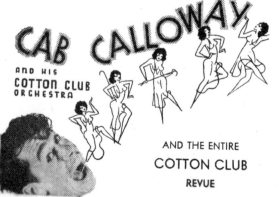

CAB CALLOWAY
AND HIS COTTON CLUB ORCHESTRA

AND THE ENTIRE
COTTON CLUB
REVUE

with the great
COTTON CLUB Cast:

Nicholas Bros.
Meers & Meers
Lethia Hill
Swann & Lee
Dynamite Hooker
Bill Bailey
Lena Horne
Cora La Redd
Cotton Club
Chorus

Two

"I'm going to make something of myself some day."

THE GREAT DEPRESSION may have taken the shine off the Harlem Renaissance, but music and art always survive. Hardship can often inspire people to create beauty and fun, taking a bite out of sadness and despair. There were plenty of street entertainers in Harlem during the Depression. Ella became one of them. She was just fifteen years old and alone, living on the streets, sometimes even ducking into movie theaters at night to be able to sleep inside. Somehow she managed to get by, at times simply accepting the kindness of strangers. "She [stayed] with people she talked to, and she ate with them, she slept wherever she could," Charles Linton—who was instrumental in getting Ella her first job—told *New York Times*

The first time Ella's name appeared in an ad was on this February 15, 1935, Harlem Opera House revue poster.

reporter Nina Bernstein years later. Ella spent her time in an area around 130th Street known then as "Black Broadway" amongst other street performers. She would dance for passersby who might have a few coins to toss her way. Ella also hung out near some of the clubs she and Charles had gone to just a few years earlier.

Around the time Ella went back to Harlem, the Apollo Theater reopened under new management after having been shut down in 1932. The Apollo, at 253 West 125th Street, was a bit farther downtown than the Savoy and the Cotton Club, and it happened to be in an all-white, mainly Irish neighborhood—a white pocket surrounded by black communities. When the Apollo reopened, it became the first theater to purposely put on shows that would appeal to black audiences in that neighborhood. This single act effectively desegregated the area.

A lot of the clubs had amateur nights, and the Apollo began holding one on Wednesdays. Ralph Cooper, who was the emcee at the Apollo, publicized their amateur nights to the people in the Apollo audiences, and advertised in local papers. The Apollo set up a system that quickly became very popular. The amateur contenders would perform, and the people in the audience would weigh in on whether they would stay or go. If the audience booed, a performer was booted off the stage. The acts that remained would get back onstage at the end of the night and take their bows one by one. Whichever group got the most applause won. Cooper said, "We decided that the winners would be awarded something better than prize money. . . . [They were] given a week's engagement at the Apollo Theater." In this way, the Apollo launched many a hopeful entertainer.

Ella and two friends decided to perform at one of the Apollo amateur nights. Now, just because she set her mind to doing it, didn't mean the prospect wasn't terrifying. Many performers were intimidated by getting up on the popular Apollo stage and offering themselves up to the demanding and highly vocal audiences there. But she persevered. "'I'm going to make something of myself one day.' That's exactly what she used to say, and she said it quite often," Charles Gulliver recalled.

Ella was no different that Wednesday night. It was November 21, 1934. In an interview with conductor

André Previn, Ella talked about that night, and what was going through her head as she watched the last act of the main show. "We used to go down to the Apollo on amateur night and there were two sisters, who were the dancingest sisters in the world, called the Edwards Sisters, and they were starring at the Apollo . . . and when I saw those ladies dance I said, 'No way I'm going out there to try and dance!'"

As the Edwards Sisters closed the main show and Ella prepared to be the first amateur onstage, she made a last-minute choice. She decided not to dance. Instead, she would sing. She had a bit of a false start when her voice faltered, but Cooper let her begin again. She sang "Judy" and "Object of My Affection." In his book *Amateur Night at the Apollo*, Cooper recalled telling the audience, "Folks hold on now. This young lady's got a gift she'd like to share with us tonight. She's just having a little trouble getting it out of its wrapper. Let's give her a second chance." Norma Miller was in the audience at the Apollo for Ella's amateur debut. "And now this child walks out onstage, tacky, out of shape, pigeon-toed . . . she was far from chic. So we started booing, y'know, like the bunch of rowdy kids we were. . . . And then she started singing. . . . She had a way of just putting it right in the pocket, and she quieted down this rowdy bunch of people."

Ella's voice mesmerized people. Charles Gulliver could hardly believe the first time he heard Ella sing. "I was so surprised when she sang, that I couldn't believe she had a voice like she has, because she always liked to dance." Her decision to sing instead of dance that particular night was one that would change the entire course of her life.

But first, there would be a few bumps in the road. Although the Apollo crowd went wild for her and Ella won the competition that night, she was never offered the weeklong gig. Her appearance, with her clunky men's boots and ill-fitting clothes, was too dirty and unkempt from living on the streets. Ella didn't seem to lose heart, though. Maybe it was out of necessity, or because people like jazz legend Benny Carter— who heard her sing that night at the Apollo and arranged an (unsuccessful) audition for her—kept her confidence up. She pressed on even after a disastrous amateur night the following month at the soon-to-be-closed Lafayette Theater, when she didn't sing well and the audience booed her. Her persistence, though, was about to pay off big-time.

The Harlem Opera House opened under new management in June 1934. The new owners, Leo Brecker and Frank Schiffman, wanted to give the Apollo a run for their money. It was partly the success of the Apollo that had caused the Lafayette—also run by Brecker and Schiffman—to fold. The Harlem Opera House was just down the street from the Apollo, and it started holding an almost identical amateur night—with the same promise of a gig as the main prize—on Tuesday nights. In January 1935, Ella took her shot on the Harlem Opera House stage and brought the house down once again. Her first-prize win was even mentioned in the *New York Age*—the first time her name ever appeared in the paper. The prize was awarded and she appeared for a week in February. She didn't walk away from the gig with any money, though. The most likely reason for this is that Schiffman probably needed to buy new, clean clothes for her to wear onstage and took it out of her pay. So Ella continued living hand to mouth on the streets.

The following month, the Chick Webb Band was preparing to perform once again at the Harlem Opera House, a venue they played often. Webb had worked his way up on the jazz scene and was now both a bandleader and an incredible drummer. He had had some shortcomings as a bandleader, because he wasn't a particularly savvy businessman and had lost some band members to other groups. Webb also had health problems. Childhood tuberculosis had deformed his spine, but he was determined to make a splash. When he began to be managed by Moe Gale, one of the founders and owners of the Savoy Ballroom, things began looking up. Gale worked out a record deal for Webb with Decca Recording Company, and was a man who would come to play a huge part in boosting both Webb's and Ella's careers.

While Webb was extremely popular in Harlem, he yearned to break into the larger market. The manager of the Savoy, Charlie Buchanan, advised Webb that he needed to add a girl singer to his band. Webb already had a male singer named Charles Linton with whom he was very happy. Some say he wasn't thrilled about the idea of adding a female singer, but reportedly, he agreed. In March 1935, Webb and Gale asked Linton to check around. Linton said, "We were opening up at the Harlem Opera House. . . . I did the classics and the ballad tunes, and they wanted me to find someone that I liked to do the swing tunes."

Beauty was one of the criteria for a girl singer. They wanted someone who was attractive. When Linton asked a girl he knew at the Opera House if she knew "of a beautiful girl who does swing tunes," she said she didn't, but that there was "that little girl who won first prize at the Apollo, and her name's Ella." Well, finding her proved tricky, since she was homeless. Linton told the girl to be on the lookout for this Ella and to let him know if she found her. A few days later, the girl brought Ella to Linton, and Ella sang for him. He brought her to meet Chick Webb.

At first, the audition didn't get off the ground. Webb didn't even want to hear her sing, she was so disheveled. He said to Linton, "You're not puttin' that on my bandstand. No, no, no." When he couldn't get Webb to listen, something clicked in Linton. For whatever reason, he took a stand as Webb and the others began to walk out of the room. "If you don't listen to her, I will quit!" Linton later said he had no intention of quitting, but that it was the only thing he could think of to say that might stop them in their tracks. Webb gave in, and told Ella he would give her a shot when they played the Savoy, but that if the audience didn't like her, she was out.

Linton went out of his way to be generous toward Ella and help her prepare. Perhaps he felt responsible after taking the risk he had, and he wanted to help make sure things worked out. Maybe, as Webb and Gale soon would, he simply had a soft spot for a lonely young girl with a beautiful voice who had no place to go. Since Ella was still homeless, Linton arranged for her to stay in a room above where he was living. He had her watch the band while they finished their engagement at the Harlem Opera House so she would be well prepared for their upcoming stint at the Savoy. Linton even offered to cover her tab at a local restaurant so she would be able to eat even if things didn't go well at the Savoy and Ella didn't go on the road with them.

But Ella did them all proud at the Savoy, knowing instinctively both how to sing and how to present herself onstage. "When he brought her to the Savoy Ballroom, well, it was a foregone conclusion. She fitted that spot like a glove," Norma Miller said. She also showed what a hard worker she was. She didn't forget her lyrics, she was always ready when the band needed her, but in the beginning she was a diamond in the rough. After years without any parental guidance or healthy living conditions, she needed to learn how to take care of herself. Her new friends even had to teach her rudimentary hygiene skills, as she smelled like she hadn't been bathing. According to Linton, Sandy Williams, a trombonist in the band, "took care of her like a father, and I mean take care. She didn't use soap and water. That's what I'm talking about." The other guys in the band called her Sis and gave her suggestions about her hair and clothes. Saxophonist Edgar Sampson said, "We all kidded her. It would always be 'Hey, Sis, where'd you get those clothes?' . . . But she always took it in good spirits."

It is hard to know whether it hurt her pride to take all this advice or not, but it is easy to imagine Ella must have felt a major sense of relief to be off the streets and have an opportunity to do something she loved. She was still young and had a sweet, naïve sense about her, despite the difficulties she had already endured. She would keep this quality throughout her life, endearing herself to many.

Within two weeks, Ella was working for Webb, which made Moe Gale her manager, too. She was just seventeen years old. Once she was on the payroll, Gale put her up in a proper room at the Braddock Hotel. Many stories circulated over the years that Chick Webb adopted Ella and took her in to live with him, but it wasn't true. Webb and his wife didn't have the room to spare, for one thing. But those stories might have been planted to make sure no one mistakenly got the idea that Ella and Webb were romantically involved, especially given her young age.

As already noted, many stories in the press about Ella's life were riddled with incorrect information. So much so, that Leslie Gourse, in her book *The Ella Fitzgerald Companion: Seven Decades of Commentary*, decided to compile original newspaper and magazine articles verbatim, accompanied by explanatory notes that point out some of the errors. For example, in an October 1940 article published in a New York daily newspaper, Malcolm Johnson talks about the band and gives a brief and quite inaccurate look at Ella's younger years. He writes that she "spent most of her childhood in an orphanage," that Webb "discovered her one night in an amateur contest at the Harlem Opera House" during which the "judges gave her the gong," and that "Webb, who was in the audience, didn't agree with the judges . . . and offered her a job." The following year, in the *New York Post*, Mark Murphy reports a similar inaccurate story. He writes, "She appeared one night on a Harlem amateur program. . . . Chick Webb, it happened, was in the audience and although the rest of the audience didn't think much of the chunky girl on stage, he liked that scared voice."

These versions of what happened to Ella are not correct, but it is interesting to see how misinformation about her history was perpetuated once it was in the public record, shrouding Ella's life in a bit of mystery. But regardless of the stories surrounding Ella and Chick Webb's relationship, it is certain that she was in good hands with the Chick Webb Band, and was about to embark on a long and glorious singing career.

Three

"She came into this business swinging."

JUST A FEW months after signing with Webb, in June 1935, Ella received her first review in the press. George Simon, from *Metronome* magazine—one of the most important music industry magazines of the time—had gone to the Savoy to hear the Chick Webb Band in May. He said he was "so knocked out by her, knocked out not only by the way she sang but the spirit and the way she would lead the band by throwing kicks on the side of the bandstand." He wrote in *Metronome*, "Miss Fitzgerald should go places." This first positive mention in the news made Ella enamored of Simon for life. If he was ever present when she was singing, she would make time to point him out to the crowd and say hello.

It didn't take long for Webb to know he had made the right move. Ella was Webb's ticket to the big-time. Focusing mostly on instrumental jazz with some vocals with Charles Linton hadn't taken Webb where he wanted to go. But now, with Ella on board, Webb watched crowds respond to her singing and knew if he included more vocal numbers he could attract a larger audience. That's exactly what he did.

He also started taking her into the Decca recording studio, beginning on June 12, 1935. Ella recorded "Love and Kisses" that summer, and the new commercial dance sound did attract a wider group of listeners. Publicist and jazz journalist Helen Oakley-Dance worked for Moe Gale for a while, helping manage Chick Webb. She said that Webb "began to see that there could be a commercial future for the band." Ella reminisced fondly about hearing her first recording. "After we made ['Love and Kisses'] . . . the band was in Philadelphia one night when they wouldn't let me in at some beer garden where I wanted to hear it on the jukebox. So I had some fellow who was over twenty-one go in and put a nickel in while I stood outside and listened to my own voice coming out."

Ella had a natural-born talent and was a quick study, much to the amazement of her peers. Nobody really knew where she had picked up sight-reading—the ability to look at, or "read," musical notes and know what notes to sing or play. Perhaps it was from the few piano lessons she may have had, or her early church singing. But she had acquired the knack from somewhere. Trumpet player Mario Bauza said, "She knew exactly what she had to do. She was smart. Give her a piece of sheet music, and she'd read it." Band member Teddy McRae said, "She could sight-read better than any of the singers. She was real fast. . . . I was thinking to myself, now how many songs has she got in her?"

The hot jazz music of the time was called swing, and Ella sure had the rhythm for it. Between her work ethic and her innate sense of timing—whether he meant it as a play on words or not—drummer Hal Austin hit the nail on the head when he said, "She came into this business swinging."

Her fellow musicians were not the only ones Ella was winning over with her voice. Her first year touring with Webb, Ella traveled to many cities, including Baltimore, Boston, Indianapolis, Chicago, Pittsburgh,

Philadelphia, Nashville, and Washington, D.C. She was a hit with the crowds from the start. And the Savoy especially—the band's home when they weren't traveling—was not an easy sell. It was a hot spot, with its beautiful mahogany floor, over-the-top elegance, and the best bands on the stage. If the people who came to dance there didn't like you, well, you knew it! Ella they loved. *Down Beat* magazine reported people "at the Savoy Ballroom were mad about her."

But not everyone was thrilled with Ella's sudden success. Most singers had to pay their dues doing small nightclub gigs for a long time before catching the kind of break that Ella did. She had seemingly appeared out of the blue and was now thrust in the spotlight. One singer, Billie Holiday, did not seem happy for the competition.

Billie Holiday shared a few things in common with Ella. She, too, had had a troubled childhood, and had been sent to a home for being truant from school. She sang for tips in Harlem nightclubs for a few years in the early 1930s, until being discovered by John Hammond. Hammond got Holiday decent club dates for pay and

Ella holds her sheet music while singing onstage in Asbury Park, New Jersey, in 1938.

recording work with famed clarinetist Benny Goodman. Holiday had certainly paid her dues, and perhaps Holiday's take was that Ella had not, having gone from obscurity to singing for Webb in one single step. Of course, this was not really the case, but it might have looked that way from where Holiday stood.

Tastes vary, and Holiday's resentment toward Ella may have been due to the fact that Teddy Wilson liked Ella's style more than Holiday's. Where Ella sang sweet like honey, Holiday had a sad, raspy tone that could make a grown man cry. Teddy Wilson was a pianist who made great jazz recordings. He had been using Holiday for vocals. When Holiday went on the road and Wilson needed a singer, he called in Ella. Holiday likely did not appreciate Ella standing in for her and may have been irked when Ella's records sold equally well. Holiday voiced her opinion of her rival on at least one occasion. Coming into the Savoy and seeing Ella onstage with Chick Webb's band she remarked with a nasty tone, "A great band like that with Ella. That b----." And with that, she turned and walked out of the place.

Ella—with her frequent work at the Savoy, in the

recording studio, and traveling on the road with the band—was gaining experience at a rapid rate. *Metronome*'s George Simon was following her progress. In January 1936, he wrote, "What a future . . . a great natural flair for singing . . . extraordinary intonation. . . . There's no reason why she shouldn't be just about the best in time to come."

Ella, as Simon noted, had work ahead of her, but she was well on her way. One way to understand what he meant and how singers mature is to look at the kinds of songs they are able to sing well. When Ella started out, Webb mainly had her singing swing tunes and other fast, catchy numbers, even though she kept asking to sing ballads. But ballads are slow and complex and require a singer to have a mature and steady control of her voice. In later years, Ella remembered Webb's early advice to her: "When I first started singing, I wanted to sing a ballad. And he didn't feel that I was prepared to sing a ballad. And without me even realizing it, with experience, as I went along singing with the band, I gradually . . . start doing ballads, and I didn't even realize that I had changed." Ella was working hard, and it showed onstage. Recordings between

June and October 1936 also showcased her growth as a singer, both in continuing to learn to control the power of her voice—which is something singers learn over time—and in her style. Those recording sessions resulted in hits on the record charts.

Benny Goodman, successful clarinetist and band leader, was one of the people who began noticing Ella—not just as the girl singer for the Webb band, but for the rising star she was. Jazz critic Leonard Feather quoted Ella in his book *From Satchmo to Miles*. "Things went so good that by the fall of 1936 Benny Goodman had me make some records with the band for Victor. But Chick was under contract to Decca, and they made them call the records back in." That is, Goodman's move to have Ella sing for him on a record for the Victor label was a conflict because Ella was with the Webb band, and Webb had an exclusive contract with Decca, so the released Victor records ended up being recalled. Ella also appeared on Goodman's radio show, and he tried to buy her contract from Webb, with no success. After the attempted buy-out, people started clamoring after her.

Ella's affiliation with Goodman was what apparently led to her dating Goodman's saxophonist Vido Musso. She reportedly became pregnant and left Webb's band for a few months to terminate the pregnancy and recover. In the meantime, Chick took the band on the road, and Teddy Hill's band took their place at the Savoy. When Ella was better, she joined the Hill band until Webb returned to New York.

It is hard to know how success can affect people. Ella's popularity was gaining momentum, but it is entirely possible that she still felt insecure. After all, she was a young woman who had been given a big break and whose star was climbing rapidly. It isn't too difficult to put yourself in her shoes and feel like you have a lot to lose at any given moment. Although she had gotten along well with the band members from the start, there were signs of some tension now.

Charles Linton remembered an instance in which they both wanted to sing a particular song. Apparently, Ella had a bit of a fit. "I liked the song first, you know. And then she wanted to do it, and then I wind up letting her do it. . . . She got a little pushy, you know what I mean? So when she gets like that, she always has her way." Drummer Mel Lewis also complained about Ella blaming band members for a performance of hers that made her unhappy. During the early years of the group, another band member, Ram Ramirez, said, "She's not as nice as people say or think that she is."

Ella, whether brusque or sweet, pulled her weight for the band. Throughout 1936, they worked the Savoy and went on the road. In March of that year, they even played an event at Yale University in New Haven, Connecticut. By 1937, Webb had eight live spots a week on the radio, featuring both Linton and Ella. They did three of them from the Savoy, and the others at Radio City Music Hall. The radio shows were national, which meant widespread exposure for the band. People all over the country were starting to know who Ella was now. The more Webb showcased popular songs, the more he used Ella. Webb was pulling in thousands of fan letters a week. Webb and Ella were a huge audience draw.

Ella agreed with Webb's decision to highlight popular songs. Her interest was in making money at this thing she loved to do. This meant that their song choices were sometimes criticized by people who took a more purist approach to jazz. So be it. Webb, along with arranger and saxophonist Teddy McRae, worked out a plan with song publisher Jack Robbins. Publishers like Robbins owned the rights to songs they bought from songwriters and stood to make more money if those songs became popular. So Robbins agreed to feed Webb the hottest songs before anyone else got their hands on them so that Ella could sing those songs and help make Robbins a success in the process. It was good for all involved. McRae said, "So he [Robbins] began to give us all these top songs. And we began to move Ella Fitzgerald . . . into pop. . . . We were going commercial."

Some people also felt as though Webb was turning his back on his black roots and going for the more commercial "whiter"-sounding songs produced by Robbins. Music critic Dave Dexter said, "The Webb band never sounded really black." And although John Hammond had great admiration for Webb and Ella both, he wrote in *Down Beat* that Webb's music choices were "badly written 'white' arrangements." Regardless of the criticisms, Webb's plan worked, catapulting Ella and the Chick Webb Band into widespread fame.

Ella was put in the spotlight much more often than

most female band singers. It was an unusual move at a time when the "girl singer" of a band was often there either just to have someone with a pretty voice and a pretty face to look at, or as an afterthought for a band. Instead, Ella was the main event. Some people criticized Webb for this. After all, this was the heyday of instrumental big-band music, and Webb was one of the great talents of the industry. He was known for his Battle of the Bands competitions, in which two bands would compete to see which one would outdo the other and be deemed the hottest. This highlight was made even better by the Savoy's double-stage setup, where dueling bands could go all out without having to stop to break down and set up new stage configurations. Helen Oakley-Dance weighed in, later saying, "The band played a smaller role, and its character was changing. I used to argue with Chick about it all the time, but he was committed to going his own way."

Ella was now making enough money to move into a nice apartment and hire a maid. It was quite an accomplishment from where she had been just a few short years before. She chose a building where some of the other musicians lived. Her next move was uptown to Seventh Avenue and 142nd Street, to be near Jo Jones. He was a drummer in Count Basie's band with a bright, wide smile and an eye for Ella. She fell for him and moved to the Woodside Hotel, a famous haunt for jazz musicians, where they often played into the wee hours of the morning. Although the romance didn't last long, the hotel's name—along with all the partying that went on there—was immortalized in a Count Basie hit called "Jumpin' at the Woodside." Ella was enjoying herself, socializing after hours more than she would later in life. Charles Linton remembered, "We used to go to nightclubs. When she came out in the morning, she would have the shoes hanging across her shoulders, and as we were walking down the street, she was walking barefoot."

In stark contrast to when she was a girl, men like Jones began to be drawn to Ella. It was not because of her looks—she had begun to put on too much weight and was self-conscious about it—but because of her talent and presence. Webb's bass player, Beverly Peer, said, "She was always with some man. All the good-looking guys hung around her because she could sing." One of the men who pursued her during the few months the Webb band played Levaggi's in Boston was President Roosevelt's son. He showed up each night with his chauffeur and drove her home.

Regardless of all the changes happening with the Webb band, Chick had certainly not given up on the Battle of the Bands nights he loved so much. They remained extremely important to him, and he continued to make time for these events amidst his more mainstream career. One battle in particular, which took place on May 11, 1937, went on to be remembered by many. This one was between the Webb band and the scorching hot Benny Goodman band. More than four thousand people crowded into the Savoy that night, with thousands more waiting in the street, hoping for a chance to get in. The police and fire departments were called to maintain order.

Webb had his sights set on beating Goodman since the battle he had lost to Duke Ellington's band back in March. Edward Kennedy "Duke" Ellington was one of the most well-known and respected pianists, composers, and band leaders of his time (or any time, for that matter). When the May battle against Goodman was upon them, Webb told Ella, "This is the turning point of this band. You know how much this means to me." Mario Bauza says he told the band, "Anybody that misses notes . . . don't come back to work!"

Webb's band won the battle that night and *Metronome*'s George Simon reported that the highlight was "Ella Fitzgerald's singing, with the crowd locking arms and swaying to and fro before her." By November 1937, Ella had beat out her rival, Billie Holiday, in the polls. Both *Down Beat* and *Melody Maker* magazine named her Number One Female Vocalist. By the end of the year, the press began to reflect the shift in the band's focus, referring to Chick and Ella, instead of Chick Webb and his orchestra. And within a few months, Ella was dubbed the First Lady of Swing.

Four

"Anything happens to me . . . take care of Ella."

ELLA AND CHICK had a few hits on the charts by the beginning of 1938. The band was doing well, but Chick's health problems were increasing. In April, he was hospitalized for two weeks. Life on the road was taxing for anyone, but for Chick it was really problematic. "This is when that hard work began to tell on Chick, because every time we closed a stage . . . the valet had to go and pick him up and bring him off the stage," Teddy McRae remembered.

This was close to the time Ella would record "A-Tisket, A-Tasket," one of the songs most associated with her throughout her life.

Ella poses for an album cover photo.

A-Tisket, a-tasket,
a green and yellow basket,
I bought a basket for my mommie,
on the way I dropped it.

As with other events of her past, the story about the recording of this song varied. One story that circulated was that Ella and the band wanted to lift Chick's spirits, so they went to the hospital and she sang him her old favorite nursery rhyme. It so cheered him, plans were made to record it as soon as he recovered. Unfortunately, as sweet as this sounds, it never actually happened.

What did happen is that Webb had recently hired a young new music arranger named Van Alexander. Ella asked Alexander to set music to (and here was the shred of truth in the previous story) an old nursery rhyme she loved—"A-Tisket, A-Tasket"—but he turned her down because he was quite busy with other work for Webb. But she was persistent, as Ella could be. Alexander said, "She put it on the line, and told me that if I didn't do the arrangement, she'd bring in someone from the outside who would. Naturally, I didn't want to alienate Ella *or* Chick." So he agreed.

Back at the Savoy, Webb put "A-Tisket, A-Tasket" on the list of songs to perform, and it became a popular hit at the club. Ella played around with it and put her unique touches to the melody and the lyrics, such as changing "walking down the avenue" to "trucking down the avenue," which fit her style better. She was twenty-one now, but was savvy enough to have the idea of using a very girlish tone to her voice for this particular song. The result was adorable. One can hardly help but smile while listening to Ella sing it.

On May 2, 1938, Ella and Webb went into the Decca studio to make the record. Decca wasn't thrilled about recording a song based on an old nursery rhyme, and told Chick they weren't going to let him do it. So "Chick started to pack up his drums and forced the issue. If he hadn't bothered, there'd be no 'Tasket.' That was down to Chick," said Beverly Peer. Chick's instincts were dead-on. The song was a hit. On June 18, it was #10 on the charts. By the end of that month, it rose to #1. Ella even had a chance to sing it on the silver screen. She made her movie debut in 1942 playing the character of Ruby in an Abbott and Costello film called *Ride 'Em Cowboy*. Ella was wonderful, giving the rendition her best schoolgirl treatment. Watching her, you can see the child within who never wanted to grow up. Ella kept on singing that song, and by 1950, "A-Tisket" had sold more than a million copies.

"A-Tisket, A-Tasket" helped make Webb's long-standing dream come true, putting their fame over the top. Teddy McRae said, "We broke record after record. People just lined the streets." It had only been three years since Ella had signed with Webb. She had gone from a complete unknown to one of the country's most famous jazz vocalists.

The band went on the road for a series of gigs just after "A-Tisket" was recorded. A few clubs in New York City allowed both whites and blacks, but both in and out of New York, most clubs and theaters were segregated. It was the 1930s, and race was a major issue in America. Trumpet player Harry "Sweets" Edison remembered how he used to feel just before going on the road with the Count Basie band. He said, "I'd absolutely almost get sick when Count Basie would give us our itinerary to go on the road. We'd get to the Holland Tunnel and almost cry leaving New York, leaving Harlem. At that time, you know, the South, it was very segregated." There were gigs, such as the one at Fairyland Park in Kansas City, where Chick and Ella would play for all-black audiences one night and all-white audiences the next—that's just the way it was. The South was even worse than the North. There were separate drinking fountains, bathrooms, train cars, and building entrances. Often, black performers had to go in the service entrance of a building instead of through the main door. Ella and her fellow black musicians were not free to eat or sleep where they liked. Traveling was often difficult in the face of segregation.

A trumpet player in Webb's band, Taft Jordan, said, "One time in Columbia, Tennessee, [we] had to go to the back of the place [to get served food] then the police came along and made 'em stop." But at least some headway was being made. For example, in September 1938, they were only the third black band to play at the Paramount Theatre in New York. And in January 1939, Chick and Ella were the first black band in years to be booked at the upscale Cocoanut Grove club in Manhattan's Park Central Hotel.

The talent Ella and Chick had was stronger than discrimination. They remained on the charts with top-selling hits. And while Ella excelled at the swing style that was so popular, she still needed more practice with the slower ballads. But she did deliver some wonderful ballads on a May 1939 radio show with the band, broadcast from their gig at the Southland Café in Boston. Carter Harman later reported in the *New York Times* that "band men who play with Ella Fitzgerald have been heard to say they tune up to her voice, so true is it." An interesting comment from one of her beaus, baritone saxophonist Heywood Henry, also reflects how a singer had to be exceptional to overcome the attitude musicians at that time had of a girl singer as a nice "extra" rather than an equal to the instrumental musicians. He said, "The guys in the band didn't pay her much attention until 'A-Tisket, A-Tasket' came along. Nobody thought much of her singing, but she was a natural! Not to learn it, just a natural, just like Frank Sinatra." Sadly, that Boston radio show was one of the last gigs Ella would do with Chick.

He had been hospitalized again in April. After Southland, he and the group went on a grueling road trip packed with gigs. But Webb was getting weaker and weaker. Knowing he wasn't doing well, he told Teddy McRae, "Anything happens to me . . . take care of Ella. Don't let the guys mess up. Just take care of Ella." By June 9, he was back in the hospital. After long-term suffering with tuberculosis, Chick Webb died on June 16, 1939.

Ella was devastated. She sang a soulful rendition of "My Buddy" at his funeral in Baltimore, Maryland. Baltimore was Webb's hometown, and the locals turned out in full force to say good-bye. Traffic was shut down throughout the city, and thousands of people attended the funeral. In Leonard Feather's book *From Satchmo to Miles*, Moe Gale is quoted as saying, "It was the biggest funeral I had ever seen—and I know there wasn't a dry eye when Ella sang." Ted Yates later reported Ella saying about Chick, "He was the kind that comes once every 1,000 years . . . always thinking of others, and always in pain, but no one ever knew it. If he'd have taken the same time that he applied to helping people, and rested he'd have lived longer than his 29 years."

The band carried on without him, fulfilling their obligations and reworking things in order to deal with the absence of Chick. They played the Savoy, went on tour through the South and Midwest, and made their way back to New York to play the Roseland Ballroom. Ella was still under contract to Gale, who wanted Webb's band to be renamed Ella Fitzgerald and Her Famous Orchestra, which it was. But being a bandleader is a job that carries a variety of responsibilities with it, including having a good business sense and knowing how to continually handle bookings for the band, deal with personnel issues, and so on. It was not a job that Ella was prepared to take over, so it would be mainly in name only that she was in charge. Benny Carter had already offered to run the show, but he wanted the band to be renamed for him, and Gale did not agree. Taft Jordan had tried his hand at it, but it wasn't his strength. Finally, Teddy McRae agreed to lead the band, with Ella as the namesake.

Ella's career and song choices up to this point had been driven by how well a song would sell rather than what artistic merit it might have—and with good results. In 1940, she joined the American Society of Composers, for composing songs such as "I Found My Yellow Basket" and "Spinnin' the Webb." Unlike most of the bigger bands of the time that evolved in style and artistry, Ella's band stayed somewhat the same, driven by her voice and chart-making hits. The success of the first three recordings after Webb's death—"Betcha Nickel," "I Want the Waiter," and "Stairway to the Stars"—indicated that the band would be okay without him.

But while Ella's popularity was climbing ever higher, some of the attention she was attracting wasn't necessarily good for her. Ella had already had several romantic relationships that hadn't worked out. For a few months around the time "A-Tisket" was recorded, she dated a saxophonist named Louis Jordan, who was married. He left the Webb band soon after their involvement ended. The following year she started dating saxophonist Heywood Henry. When Ella appeared onstage one night sporting a diamond engagement ring, the press went wild. According to Heywood, it was a bit of a publicity stunt spontaneously concocted by Ella. She happened to be wearing a ring, and when a reporter asked her about it, she said Henry had given it to her. Henry said, "Later she sent me a telegram saying did I mind. . . . I sent her one back saying it didn't make any difference. . . . It wasn't the truth, but we were going around together." But it was Ella's relationship with a man named Benny Kornegay in 1941 that caused her some real trouble.

Kornegay used to hang around her concerts. "That's who she went off with in between shows," Beverly Peer said. Kornegay even started riding the bus with the band to be close to Ella. Then he moved in with her. All might have been fine if Kornegay had been a decent guy, but that turned out not to be the case. In the beginning, he had made a good show of things by being generous and paying for things—sometimes dinner for the whole group that was out. But it soon appeared he had money troubles, and he leaned on Ella for help. She gave it, as her judgment was clouded by her feelings for him. When he asked her to marry him, she said yes. They hadn't known each other long when they married on December 26, 1941.

Moe Gale had his suspicions about Kornegay and looked into his background in order to protect Ella. It was a good thing he did. Gale turned up evidence that Kornegay had a criminal past and advised Ella to separate from him. But Ella was already spinning lovely stories to the press about how wonderful their relationship was and how supportive her new husband could be. She told a reporter that "We just started our apartment and I want to get into the kitchen," and that Benny was content to listen to her albums while she was traveling on the road. After a few weeks, Gale managed to make her see the light, but Kornegay did not want to grant Ella a divorce. They went to court to get the marriage annulled. Ella later—and incorrectly—reported that the judge had told her, "You just keep singing 'A-Tisket, A-Tasket' and leave these men alone."

As with other incidents in her life, Ella was simply determined to put the whole episode behind her and go on with the show, as Chick had taught her. People who knew her have remarked on her ability to forget the past, such as how she always glossed over the troubled pieces of her childhood. In fact, some sources even disagreed as to whether or not her marriage to Kornegay ever occurred in the first place, partly because Ella herself professed to be fuzzy on the details and would sometimes cite his first name as Barney. But the existence of a marriage license between Ella Fitzgerald and Benjamin Kornegay confirms it as fact. Perhaps Ella simply would have preferred to forget it, and that's perfectly understandable. "She wanted somebody to be nice to her, but her first marriage was a disaster," Norma Miller said.

At this time, Ella's career was by no means a disaster, but it was faltering a bit. Although her live performances continued to be filled with soul and style, her recordings were not as satisfying. Her ratings began to slip. *Metronome* had named her the Number One Female Vocalist in 1940. But in 1941, her ranking fell to seven. Much of this likely had to do with Gale's shortsighted management of Ella. She recorded more than twenty songs that year, but Gale kept her recording mostly popular songs, such as "The Muffin Man" and "Keep Cool, Fool." But although these were songs that did fine commercially, they didn't encourage her growth as an artist. It wasn't only Gale's fault. Ella could have exhibited more of a discriminating taste for songs that would have made her shine as brightly as she could have, songs that would have challenged her to stretch herself as a singer.

Meanwhile, the band continued to tour, but there

was growing resentment about how Gale treated them. Taft Jordan said, "The higher-ups . . . didn't want to pay anybody any money. I think we were making $75 a week while guys in other big orchestras that were not drawing as much as we were were making $25 to $35 a week more." While the band was touring, recording, and working their hearts out, they were not earning enough. Moreover, the band did not enjoy traveling on a bus, but Gale wouldn't spring to send them by train. He even made them pay for their own hotel rooms and band uniforms! When it was Webb fronting the band, loyalty to him had sustained a lot of the band members. But now that Gale was really running the band strictly as a business, unhappiness grew. Teddy McRae went to the mats with Gale, saying, "Look, give the guys a raise. This band should get more money!" Gale's response was to fire him. He then hired Eddie Barefield, but the problems didn't change. By the end of July 1942, Chick Webb's band was no longer together.

Five

"Come on up and do it with the fellas."

EVEN BEFORE THE group known as Ella Fitzgerald and Her Famous Orchestra disbanded, Moe Gale had Ella make a few recordings with one of his other acts called the Three Keys, which consisted of three brothers who sang and played bass, piano, and guitar. *Down Beat* said of their May 1942 effort, "Best Ella's done in some time but what a difference in her style! As compared with her singing with the Webb band, she's softened down, dropped her jump phrasing, and become almost a ballad singer." And although Ella enjoyed singing ballads, this was not intended as a compliment. The critic was implying that Ella had lost her edge.

In August 1942, a record she had made with her

orchestra was released. *Down Beat* did give it some praise, but the magazine also said, "The driving power that made Ella a great singer seems to have trickled away." In September 1942, Ella and the Three Keys gave a live performance in New York, at the Aquarium Theatre. They went on to tour for the next few months, hitting clubs and theaters in New York, Boston, Washington, D.C., Baltimore, Detroit, and Chicago.

Gale was positioning Ella more as a solo artist now. It should have been an easy transition to make for a talent like hers. The United States had been involved in World War II since December 1941, which put a sadder tone on things, lessening the desire people had for listening to big-band swing music. Wartime rations had made travel hard as well as expensive, which affected both touring groups and concertgoers. In addition, the American Federation of Musicians, the labor union for professional musicians, told their members to stop making new records to put pressure on record companies to pay the artists more. Since singers did not belong to the union, Ella was still able to record. One might think Decca would have snapped her up, but they didn't, due to her drop in popularity.

Billie Holiday's more sentimental, sad tone seemed to suit people better around this time, along with crooners such as Frank Sinatra. In his book *First Lady of Song*, author Geoffrey Mark Fidelman quotes an unnamed friend of Ella's commenting that her popularity was on the decline: "This was a low point for her, she really didn't know how to take it." Ella was still a favorite of the club scene, but she needed something to get her overall career back on track, especially after the Three Keys broke up when the men were sent off to war. In September 1943, the Decca recording company satisfied the musicians' union requests for better deals. Two months later, Decca's record producer Milt Gabler got Ella back into the studio with some musicians. (It's helpful to note the way the music business worked at that time. Ella was under contract both to Moe Gale—her manager—and Decca, her recording label. Gabler was in charge of handling Ella's work for Decca.)

Meanwhile, Gale had been sending Ella on a solo-gig circuit. She often traveled with only her cousin Georgiana Henry, who traveled with her for years, assisting her on the road. Gale would arrange for Ella to sing using local musicians as backup at the various places they stopped. Gabler was upset. "I never liked the way Moe Gale handled Ella. I went to New Jersey one night to see her. . . . The musicians' dressing room was up the stairs and up at the back, and there were no screens. . . . There was nobody to check the amplification or the balance of the little group that was going to play with her. . . . A great talent like that, and [he] didn't send a roadman to make sure she was treated properly." But in January 1944, Gale put together a proper lineup of musicians and sent Ella on the road to the big theaters. Six months later, during a stop in New York on another leg of Gale's tour, Gabler arranged for Ella to have some time in the recording studio again.

Gabler had control over what songs Ella would sing on Decca. "When I started handling Ella, I made the decision what the company would invest in as a record—tunes, treatments," he said. In an interview, Gabler explained how the industry worked. "Singers didn't make too many decisions about what they recorded. It had to do with music publishers. We made the decision what actual songs we were going to invest in." Gabler knew what he was doing. In August 1944, he recorded "Into Each Life Some Rain Must Fall" and "I'm Making Believe" with Ella, and both songs hit #1 right off the bat. *Down Beat* said, "She's never done anything quite like it, and her vocal is actually thrilling." Gabler produced several more hits for Ella, and her popularity began to climb again.

Although Ella was a singer with no formal training, she was a pro at learning as she went. Ella's musical instincts were dead-on. The more she sang, the better she got. Arts critic Howard Reich later said of Ella, "Her art was hard won, with the singer transforming herself from naïve beginner to master musician through unrelentingly hard work." Ella's technique was improving, her style was evolving, and she was better than ever.

Ella and the rest of Gale's lineup were back on the road in the fall. It was still wartime, and public transportation was widely used and often crowded. And in the South, segregation was still commonplace. There were blacks-only and whites-only cars on the train. You can imagine how a large group of black musicians traveling in this way would run into their share of problems. Dancer Norma Miller, who toured with bands at that time, remembered how hard it was to get service: "We couldn't get a hamburger. . . . Up to this day, I'm mad with everybody." Harry "Sweets" Edison, who toured with Count Basie's band, recalled the atmosphere, too: "We used to take pictures of signs 'For colored only,' 'For whites only,' even drinking fountains."

One day when Ella was on the road, there were no available seats in the blacks-only car, and she sat down in a whites-only car. The conductor tried to remove her, and he likely would have if a group of white soldiers had not intervened and told the conductor to leave her alone. In addition, the hotels available for "Coloreds" were often dirty and run-down. Ella's later response to this situation was this: "I worked with the band when we had to travel through the South. And I went through all of those experiences, so I feel great that I've been able to pay those dues, because when you pay them, then you know what it's all about. That's how we become greater, by learning to face these things." She also told *Down Beat* that, in general, traveling "isn't as easy on a woman as it is on a man. And you've heard how guys complain about the road." Teddy McRae commented on how tough it could be for a woman constantly en route with a group of men, saying that sometimes "she almost had to get dressed on the bus. It was really rough on a girl traveling with a band."

Gabler continued to fit in recording sessions with Ella when she was in New York. Next up was "And Her Tears Flowed Like Wine," which reached #10 on the charts after it was released. He followed this up with "I'm Beginning to See the Light," which hit #5. By January 1945, Ella's ratings began to climb again. And although she did get a radio spot with NBC for Saturday afternoons that ran eight weeks, there was still evidence of racial discrimination within the industry. In 1947, Metronome's Bob Bach would write, "Somehow or other she has been unable to get on the radio with a program of her own or a regular spot on a big show." After referring to several white singers who did receive steady radio coverage, he continued, "Need we draw any neon arrows to lead you to the large and disgraceful spectre of Jim Crowism behind American radio? . . . If you want one small example of the malodorous color line in radio today I will simply cite the answer I was given by one advertising bigwig when I suggested Ella for an opening on a big network show: 'She wouldn't look so good for pictures.'" (The Jim Crow laws required public places in the South to be segregated until 1964.)

Amidst the disturbing realities of race relations in the country at this time, there were still many high points for Ella. In July 1945, she graced the cover of *Down Beat* magazine. In December, she guest-starred on the nationally broadcast CBS variety radio show, *The Jack Smith Show*. It was reported that she was paid twice the amount of any other black performer to be hired for a guest spot on that show. This was a testimony to her growing fame.

In January 1946, Gabler arranged for Ella to record two songs with famed trumpeter and vocalist Louis Armstrong: "You Won't Be Satisfied" and "The Frim Fram Sauce." At this point, as historian and jazz expert Stuart Nicholson notes in his impeccable biography *Ella Fitzgerald*, "Ella had become a specialist at the jazz-influenced vocal, singing the melody relatively straight in the first chorus and embellishing it in the final one." Indeed, this would become one of her standard approaches to song. And the beauty lies in the fact that she made it all sound so effortless. A record review from *Metronome* expressed the same sentiment: "Other girl singers should listen and learn."

Ella knew exactly who to keep her ears trained on. Singer Mel Tormé said of her, "She just kept those extraordinary ears open listening to the likes of Roy Eldridge and Coleman Hawkins and Lester Young. . . . The list is endless." Tormé also remarked at her natural "God-given talent." Talent, yes, and tenacity, too. Bassist Keter Betts said, "You take these certain 'gifted' people, and the reason they rise above the others is because they're constantly sharpening their minds. . . . Ella was constantly singing to herself at all times."

When Ella had the chance to sing with the charismatic Louis Armstrong, she made the most of it, listening—and effectively training on the job. Satchmo, as he was nicknamed, was a master of scat—a style of singing in which nonsense syllables are substituted for words and a singer often improvises the melody line and phrasing in order to sound like a musical instrument. Ella was an excellent scat singer and had proven it with an all-scat version of the song "Flying Home,"

which received rave reviews. Louis and Ella riffed together—shortening and lengthening phrases, and
improvising as they went. They were fun to listen to,
breezy and upbeat, with a sense of play and a flair for
style. Ella could also affectionately mimic Louis's classic gravelly, rumbling sound. It was a quirk she used to
pay homage to Armstrong for the rest of her career.

Gale was keeping Ella busy. In addition to the bigger clubs she was doing, he was still booking her at
venues that were not the right caliber for her growing
stature—treatment that annoyed Gabler. Nicholson
writes, "Moe Gale continued to draw up tour sched-
ules that included putting Ella out as a single [without
a band]. It was lonely work . . . and for someone with
Ella's ability, it was also demeaning."

Meanwhile, Gabler was also filling Ella's schedule.
In the May 1946 issue of *Metronome*, on which Ella
appeared on the cover, a review ran of Ella's newest records with Gabler, "I Didn't Mean a Word I Said" and
"I'm Just a Lucky So and So." It said, "Ella's great phrasing, her amazing musical conceptions . . . the overall,
relaxed feel of these two sides . . . revive hope in the
revival of this great singer." That same month, she did

a weeklong run at the Apollo, which Leonard Feather reviewed. "Ella provided as many vocal thrills as ever. She has gained in poise and personality through the years without losing any of the spontaneity that is such an important part of her charm."

"Flying Home" had been a clear indication that Ella was at home with the newer bebop music that was becoming popular in the jazz world. Bebop featured quick tempos and a lot of improvisation based on harmonies rather than melodies. One of the leaders of this growing craze was trumpeter John "Dizzy" Gillespie. Dizzy had a mischievous grin and cheeks that he puffed out like a blowfish when he blew into his horn. When trumpeter Clark Terry asked Dizzy about his infamous cheek puffing for an interview in *Down Beat* magazine, Dizzy said, "I really don't know. I didn't have a teacher in my early days, but I heard things in my head I wanted to play. . . . Blowned and blowned and blowned and blowned!"

Dizzy was not only a respected musician, he was something of a character—sporting a goatee, beret, and horn-rimmed glasses that young fans liked to

Dizzy Gillespie blows his horn in his signature style, circa 1948.

copy. He had earned the nickname "Dizzy" from the
excited way he loved to experiment with music, "playing chord changes, inverting them and substituting
different notes, trying to see how different sounds led
naturally, sometimes surprisingly into others." Dizzy
often clowned around onstage—dancing during other
people's solos, making outrageous faces, or waving to
someone in the audience. Dizzy's third-grade teacher,
Alice Wilson, attests to the fact that he was consumed

by music from a young age. "He didn't care about anything but music. He would come to school every morning with his horn under his arm, instead of books," she said. Dizzy stayed on fire, always. *The New Yorker* writer and jazz critic Whitney Balliett said, "[He] never merely started a solo, he erupted into it."

In November 1946, Moe Gale sent Ella on tour with Gillespie's band. But even though Ella's bebop style had begun to develop, the guys in Dizzy's band were famous for it and still saw Ella mainly as a swing singer. They weren't convinced she would fit in. Pianist John Lewis said, "My appreciation for Ella wasn't as great as it should have been, although after Dizzy kept pointing it out to me every night, I got the message!" Ella learned a lot from Dizzy and credited him with really teaching her how to bebop. In true Ella fashion, she studied on the job. "I used to get thrilled listening to them when he did his bebop. That's actually the way I feel I learned what you call bop. It was quite an experience, and he used to always tell me, 'Come on up and do it with the fellas.' That was my education in learning how to really bop."

One of the reasons that bebop was a natural fit

for Ella was that it brought out her talent for messing around with rhythms. Previn remarked on Ella's ability to use her voice as one of the horns in the band—something she was able to really play at with Dizzy. She would function like an extension of the horn section, often mimicking back the action of a slide trombone or the melody line a horn played, twisting it and scatting it in a different variation, and the horn would then bounce that line right back to her. She credited Dizzy with teaching her how to do that: "Listening to Dizzy made me want to try something with my voice that would be like a horn. He'd shout 'Go ahead and blow!' and I'd improvise."

Ella loved playing back and forth off the horns like that. Listening to her volley with trumpeter Roy Eldridge is a thrilling ride. Both musicians sound connected or intertwined with each other. It's a joy to hear. Ella told Previn, "With the horns you get a feeling that anybody's together, and we're all for each other. . . . I think that was the greatest education I've had." In fact, her ability to imitate instruments helped her hone her unique style and become one of the best scat singers there ever was. "I think she brought scat singing to a new level of artistry," saxophonist Sonny Rollins said. As the intricate and fast-paced bebop took over swing, Ella made that transition successfully, at a time when a lot of other folks, such as clarinetist Benny Goodman, did not. "Fitzgerald did what many jazz musicians couldn't—she made a seemingly effortless transition from swing to bebop," said *Washington Post* critic Richard Harrington. This was largely due to her ability to be flexible with her style. She was not afraid to try different things with her voice and adapted well to whatever forms of music were popular.

Ella enjoyed touring with Dizzy's group. They covered a lot of ground, playing all over the eastern and southern United States, Illinois, and Texas. "We would go into the towns and go to the clubs. There'd be a nightclub or somewhere to go, and the band would start playing and we would get up and that was it! We used to take the dance floor over." Ella hadn't lost her love of dancing, and it showed.

There was a bass player from Philadelphia in Dizzy's band who sure didn't mind dancing with Ella. His name was Ray Brown. Brown was an excellent bassist who was introduced to Dizzy one night in a club by fellow musician Hank Jones. When Jones assured Dizzy that Brown was good, he simply said, "Do you want a gig?" Brown later told *Down Beat* magazine, "I almost had a heart attack. So he . . . said to be at his house tomorrow night . . . and there was Diz and Bud Powell and Max Roach and *Bird*! . . . I was in as deep as you can get." He was about to get in even deeper. Ray and Ella started spending more time together, even after the tour ended. Ella's stint with Dizzy Gillespie's band had given her a great deal: a foray into a new genre of music well suited to her voice and talents—and another chance at love.

Ray Brown and Ella, happily married in 1951.

Six

"This one pays the rent."

ON ONE OF the nights Gabler went to listen to his star singer perform in the clubs, he heard Ella do "Lady Be Good." He had a habit of saying, "'This one pays the rent' and 'This one's for us'" whenever she did a number he thought would be a hit. He knew right away he wanted to make a record of her singing that song and said, "'Lady Be Good' was for us!" They recorded it in March 1947 in just one take. It was perfect the first time. When *Down Beat* reviewed it a few months later, they gave it a rare five stars: "You saw right— *Good* drags down five notes. . . . Will be listened to just as avidly ten years from now. . . . Her intonation perfect, her instrumental conception magnificent. . . . Tersely, on this one, Ella's a hella."

To those in the know, the recent influence from Dizzy came shining through as well. Bob Bach, in *Metronome*, wrote, "'Lady Be Good' . . . represents her awareness of the Gillespie school of jazz." If there had been any doubt about Ella getting up to the top again, there wasn't anymore. She was back, full force. And "Lady Be Good" wasn't just good for Ella in the short-term—it would stay in her repertoire for the long haul. Years later, *Village Voice* jazz critic Garry Giddins wrote about Ella in 1976, saying, "She wasn't born of bop . . . but she was thoroughly accepted into the fold. . . . She thrived on it, roaring through a lexicon of bop licks on 'Lady Be Good,' which became one of her most requested and enduring showpieces."

In June 1947, the Downbeat Club opened on 52nd Street in Manhattan. Ella was asked to be the headliner, and she brought the house down. She also brought in a record-breaking $7,683 her first week there. Moe Gale, still Ella's manager, continued to book her with Dizzy Gillespie's band. In September, this included being part of the lineup to perform the night of Gillespie's debut at Carnegie Hall.

It was a big night for bebop. Joining Dizzy and

Ella in the spotlight was well-known composer and saxophonist Charlie "Yardbird" Parker, a.k.a. the Bird. Parker was already lauded for his bebop talents and had played with Dizzy plenty of times before. He had been blowing people away from his early days of playing at the Savoy. Musician Howard McGhee recalled that when "Charlie got up and played, we all stood there with our mouths open because we hadn't heard anybody play a horn like that." Pianist Jay "Hootie" McShann said, "He had a completely different approach in everything. Everything was completely different, just like [when] you change the furniture in the house and you come in and you won't know your own house." Dizzy said about Parker, "He was the other half of my heartbeat" and "sometimes I couldn't tell whether I was playing or not because the notes were so close together." Their styles were quite different, though, with Dizzy focusing more on harmony and Parker more on rhythm.

When Ella got up on that Carnegie stage with Dizzy and Bird on September 29, 1947, her star shone as brightly as ever. She wore a beautiful white evening dress and sang six songs. Among them were "Flying

Home" and "Lady Be Good." The night was a grand success—with SOLD OUT and STANDING ROOM ONLY labels slapped on the poster outside. In the *New York Times*, Carter Harman reported on the edginess of the music: "The rhythmic patterns are to one's knowledge, unique in jazz, broadening the base from the usual four beats to a space sometimes covering several bars." Jazz critics gave rave reviews. *Metronome* even said, "A new era of jazz began in 1947." The war had ended, the nation had gotten its spirits up, and a new sound was being ushered in. Dizzy wrote, "Your music reflects the times in which you live. My music emerged from the war years . . . and it reflected those times. . . . Fast and furious, with the chord changes going this way and that way, it might've looked and sounded like bedlam, but it really wasn't." Happiness was a key ingredient to bebop. Milt Jackson, one of Dizzy's musicians, recalled how it felt: "From the first note to the last note, you could hear that happiness, that togetherness, you can hear it all in that music."

It was a life-changing year for Ella. In addition to her musical life, she had gotten involved with helping needy children—a cause she would keep close to her for the rest of her years. Perhaps this came at a time when she was able to both enjoy her success and have enough distance from her past to be inspired to help other children who suffered. Her first involvement was with an organization called Foster Parents Plan, which helped disabled and orphaned children in post-war Europe. Ella sent money to pay for housing for an Italian orphan. In addition to this new aspect of Ella's life, by the end of 1947, there was an even bigger change on the horizon.

Ella and Ray Brown had been seeing each other steadily. When Ray proposed marriage, she happily accepted. The couple didn't waste any time. They went to a court in Youngstown, Ohio, while Dizzy's band was doing a gig there, and were married that same day. It was December 10, 1947. One of the reasons that Ella's birth date has been reported incorrectly over the years can be traced to her marriage certificate. She made herself a year younger—twenty-nine instead of thirty—on this document! The reason for this is not known, although many have assumed she simply wanted to be younger in the eyes of her twenty-one-year-old husband. When Ray and Ella returned to New York, they found an apartment together in Queens. But marital bliss soon hit a snag.

Dizzy's band was about to go on an extensive European tour. Meanwhile, saxophonist Illinois Jacquet, another important bandleader in the bebop movement, was heading out on tour all over the East and Midwest. Ella was booked to go on the road with Jacquet, while Ray was supposed to be with Dizzy. Understandably, Ray and Ella didn't want to be separated so soon after getting married. It appears that they tried to work things out, but Ella couldn't arrange to get time off from Jacquet's tour to go overseas and hook up with Dizzy's band. Brown said, "I was in a bit of a curl between her wanting me to travel with her as well." In the end, it seems, Brown didn't do either. "I finally decided I was going to stay in New York."

Meanwhile, Ella was on fire. Her tour with Jacquet in January and February 1948 was extremely successful. Jacquet said, "We went on tour with Ella Fitzgerald and broke all records in blizzard weather in January." At Carnegie Hall on January 17, a newspaper reported, "A capacity crowd turned out. . . . Beside selling out the house, 200 on-stage seats were sold. . . .

With tickets going at a $4.80 top, the box office reaped a few dollars less than $7,500." This was an increase from just a few months earlier, when Ella's night with Dizzy on the Carnegie stage had pulled in $5,300. The rest of her tour with Jacquet went just as well. Ella had now proven herself to Gale, who finally began booking only the best for Ella—good clubs and nice hotels. Of course, her schedule never let up. After the run with Jacquet, she went right back out on the road—for a week in Oakland, California, followed by a second week in Los Angeles. And by April, she was back in the recording studio.

In June, Ella, with Ray heading up his trio, played a monthlong stint at The Three Deuces in Manhattan. For their opening night, the crowd included such musical celebrities as Nat King Cole, Benny Goodman, and Duke Ellington—a testimony to Ella's draw, and a tribute to her success. Ella and Ray's trio were at the Apollo in August, and then on to Chicago's Rag Doll Club by the end of the month. There, she began to sing more ballads than the bebop tunes she had become famous for—and which her fans craved. This would be a thorn in her side throughout her career. She had always loved to sing ballads and, in fact, preferred to mix up her concerts in general and not just sing one type of tune. But people still begged for her hits such as "How High the Moon" and "Flying Home." *Down Beat* reported on her performance at the Rag Doll: "'I don't like to sing bop most.' . . . It was no one less than Ella Fitzgerald saying that, and if she hadn't qualified it with a 'most,' it would have shattered the illusions of thousands of her fans."

Ray and Ella got to take a honeymoon of sorts in September, when they set off with pianist Hank Jones for Ella's first tour overseas. Before the group left, a good-bye party was thrown for them at The Three Deuces. A couple of days later, they sailed for England aboard the *Queen Mary*. One of the pop songs Ella had recorded with Gabler, "My Happiness," had been released in England, so her audiences were familiar with it, and clamored for the song as an encore. Once Ella discovered this song was a hit, she included it to the crowd's delight. When she told Gabler what had happened, he was not surprised. He said, "In those years when you did something that was jazz-oriented, like those first riff tunes, it would sell maybe 180,000 to 200,000 records tops. But if you did a song like 'My Happiness,' it would sell 500,000 to 600,000 records. So I said, 'That pays for all the good things we want to do.'" In general, the English seemed to prefer her more commercial songs. But on the last night there, they were asked to perform with the wildly popular Sunday Swing Session at the Palladium, led by Ted Heath. Ella clearly enjoyed herself as she "danced and jived in front of the orchestra." She was inspired to deliver some of her best bebop performances to a crowd so enthralled it offered an "ear-splitting ovation" and begged for a half hour of encores.

Upon returning home in the first week of November, Ella went into the recording studio to make two of her last records of the 1940s: "In My Dreams" and "To Make a Mistake Is Human." Gary Giddins called her 1940s recordings the "most uneven . . . a reflection of an in-between dilemma that defined the era. Swing was losing its magic, and bop was little more than an underground workshop." It was true that, as exciting as bebop was, it didn't seem to be catching on widely enough. "Bop is a flop—commercially," *Variety* wrote in 1949. Regarding Ella's recordings, though, the inconsistent body of work from this period was partly a reflection of Decca's tendencies to sometimes focus on a song with commercial potential over one that might be considered more artistic. Giddins said, "It was Decca's policy to integrate jazz and pop. . . . The results were often charming, and just as often detestable." But even with some of the records that didn't sell as well, such as "Darktown Strutters' Ball" and "Shine," under her belt, Ella's recordings in the 1940s had also given the world "Flying Home," "How High the Moon," and the beautiful ballad "I've Got the World on a String." Ella's popularity was solid, and growing stronger all the time.

Once she had finished her work in the Decca studios, Ella and the Ray Brown trio left for a week-long gig in Detroit at the Paradise Theatre. And if the crowds in Detroit were any indication, her American fans had missed Ella while she was abroad. After Detroit, Ella and Ray's trio returned to New York to perform for two weeks at the Royal Roost with saxophonist Lester Young and his group.

* ✦ ⭐ ✦ *

Moe Gale often booked another one of his groups, the Ink Spots, with Ella, and Ella made some records with them. That group had their "first million-selling disc . . . in 1944 with 'Into Each Life Some Rain Must Fall,' performed with Ella Fitzgerald." It's not too presumptuous to conclude that Ella had something to do with their success. Bobby Schiffman, who later took over ownership of the Apollo Theater from his father, Frank, said of that time, "No jazz show was successful unless it had a major female artist headlining. . . . I have had some great pure-jazz shows with Miles Davis [and] Charlie Parker. . . . But if you don't have Ella Fitzgerald, Sarah Vaughan, or Dinah Washington as the headliner, you can forget it." Things had certainly changed since the days of the girl singer serving as pretty window dressing for the band.

In December 1948, the Ink Spots were able to do something that paved the way for all black performers, including Ella. They were booked at the Monte Carlo Club in Miami. It was the first time black artists had entertained at this nightclub, which was a big deal at the time. The crowd was crazy about them. Later, the Negro Actors Guild gave the Ink Spots a plaque to commemorate this historic achievement. Up next at the Monte Carlo was Ella. She, too, was very well

received by the audiences there, and the club continued to book black entertainers from that point on.

On February 11, 1949, Ella took the stage at Carnegie Hall. This time, she was working for a man who
would affect her life as dramatically as Chick Webb
had. Norman Granz was one of the few "non-musicians
who have shaped the course of jazz history." Granz fell
in love with jazz while in college at the University of
California at Los Angeles (UCLA). After a brief stint
in the army, he moved back to Los Angeles in 1942.

Segregation and racial discrimination in America
were certainly not limited to the South. Granz hated
the fact that the big nightclubs in Los Angeles kept
black customers out. That summer, he came up with
a plan, rounded up some musicians, and struck a deal
with the owners of a few clubs: Granz would put together jam sessions for any night of the week a club
was normally closed to give its house band a break,
thereby giving the owners a way to make up for that
lost revenue. In return, Granz required the club owners to fill the dance floor with tables so patrons would
know they were coming to listen to the music and not
just to dance. More importantly, he made them agree

to let black customers attend the shows. Granz said, "Black musicians were playing all over Los Angeles in the '40s, but almost entirely to white audiences . . . because there were very few places that welcomed blacks as patrons." Granz had an eye for talent, his bookings became extremely popular, and his plan worked, marking the beginning of his lifelong dedication to fighting racism through musical pursuits.

Two years later, in 1944, Granz approached the Los Angeles Philharmonic about putting on a jazz event for a much larger audience than a typical nightclub crowd. He wanted to bring jazz to the masses. Jam sessions were not a mainstream choice, as this more free-form style of jazz had not yet caught on. But the July 2, 1944, show sold out, and Granz's idea for Jazz at the Philharmonic (JATP) was born. He continued to put on the concerts once a month. As recordings of the concerts were released, the popularity and reputation of JATP grew. They were exciting shows, and included "The Battle," in which musicians—in the tradition of the Chick Webb Battle of the Bands—were pitted against one another to see who could win the most affection from the crowd. Granz attracted some of the best musicians in the business, and Ray Brown was one of them.

When Ella went to visit Ray during one of his performances with JATP in 1948, Granz had her come up onstage and sing. He had been following her career and wanted a regular singer on his program. He had been partial to Billie Holiday, who had done some work for him, but Holiday's drug addiction made her difficult to depend on. The crowd, of course, went wild for Ella. Granz worked out a deal with Moe Gale, who was still her manager, and contracted her for his 1949 JATP tour. But she wouldn't be able to make records for Granz's label, because her contracts with Gale and Decca prevented that. Ella opened for Granz's JATP on that momentous night in February 1949 at Carnegie Hall, thus beginning a relationship that was paramount to her career for the rest of her life.

Seven

"Norman, I love Ella just as much as you do."

THE COAST-TO-COAST JATP tour, which opened at Carnegie in February 1949 and would end on March 30, 1949, was a hit. In April, New York's newest jazz club opened. Bop City was located on Broadway, with the heady subtitle THE JAZZ CENTER OF THE WORLD in bright lights on the marquee. Artie Shaw was a critically acclaimed jazz clarinetist, composer, and bandleader. He and Ella were booked for opening night. Surprisingly, Artie Shaw brought a full orchestra and tried to perform his takes on classical music. It was not the night to experiment. After an hour and a half, and with what had become a very unhappy crowd, Ella took over and turned things around.

Ella's career was moving right along. Between her

recording deals and her nonstop live bookings, *Ebony* magazine estimated her 1949 income to be about $150,000—a tremendous amount of money for that time. Ella was making Granz proud. Although her popularity remained strong, some of her song choices seemed to be working against her. This had been a touchy subject for Granz since the beginning of their relationship. He wanted to change her roster of songs and get rid of some of the novelty selections, but he couldn't do so without permission from Gale. Now the critics were taking note. Their reviews showed how much they loved Ella's voice, despite how they felt about some of the material. "Ella Fitzgerald sang what was generally regarded as a crummy selection of songs with delicacy and personal appeal. Just how 'Old Mother Hubbard,' 'Mr. Paganini,' and 'A Little Bird Told Me' got into her repertoire we don't know," wrote *Down Beat*'s critic when the JATP hit Chicago. But Granz's hands were tied as long as Gale remained in charge of Ella's career—something Granz intended to change.

Granz was fully in the Ella fan camp at this point, and booked her for the next JATP tour that fall. Once

Ella and Norman Granz.

again, they opened at Carnegie Hall, this time on September 18. The midnight concert sold out. Granz added to Ella's program, having her not only sing her tunes but join in on the jam sessions, as well. Oh, how Ella could shine right alongside those horns! Ella had long loved to play off the horns, and this pairing quickly became a favorite with audiences. Ella was given top billing on the tour. Along with other stars who took the stage that night—such as Charlie Parker, her husband Ray Brown, and Lester Young—pianist Oscar Peterson had been brought in by Granz as a surprise guest. Ella, Peterson, and the whole evening were a smash hit. Granz would go on to manage Peterson's career and make him a major jazz celebrity. He also set his sights on making Ella's star rise even higher.

From Carnegie Hall, the JATP crew went on the road for two months. Where jazz had mainly been heard in smaller clubs, Granz brought the music to large and often elegant venues that attracted mainstream crowds. But the only crowds Granz was interested in were those that were integrated. He had no tolerance for racism and segregation, and he made his views part of the deal. It was a bold step forward, and he took it without hesitation. Granz instituted a contract that club owners had to sign promising not to segregate audiences. If they didn't sign, Granz's players didn't play. He also made sure his artists never suffered at the hands of racist behavior. "He gave jazz class," remembered Harry "Sweets" Edison. "He would have it in his contract if there was any discrimination in the hall, there was no concert. . . . He made you feel like all the bad times you have had in this business—he made you feel like you have accomplished something in your life."

Granz had all the right elements at his disposal—a deep and authentic passion against discrimination, a good heart, and the momentum of the beginning of the Civil Rights Movement. The time was right for implementing major changes. Although segregation was still in place, the 1950s were the start of some progress. In 1954, the U.S. Supreme Court, in the *Brown v. Board of Education* case, decreed that black and white children should be able to attend school together, stating that "in the field of education the doctrine of 'separate but equal' has no place. Separate educational facilities are inherently unequal." Of course, the South was slow to act on that ruling, but it was a start. In 1955, when Rosa Parks refused to give up her seat on the bus, her actions helped jump-start the Montgomery Bus Boycott that protested the segregation of blacks and whites on public buses. And the Civil Rights Act of 1957, although more symbolic than practical, prohibited anyone from interfering with an African American's right to vote.

Make no mistake, though—there was still plenty of trouble to go around. Lynchings were still occurring in the South, and the Ku Klux Klan was experiencing a boost in their numbers. Martin Luther King Jr.'s house was bombed, as were four black Baptist churches, and there was violence at the University of Alabama over black student Autherine Lucy's presence. And the North Alabama White Citizen's Council told people, "Negro music appeals to the base in man [and] brings out cannibalism and vulgarity." Members of this group went so far as to attack singer Nat King Cole when he took the stage for the first of two performances—the early one for an all-white audience, the later one for an all-black audience—in Birmingham, Alabama, in April 1956.

But Norman Granz was on a mission. He had no tolerance for racism and did what he could to even the playing field for his beloved jazz. He said, "Jazz is America's own. It is played and listened to by all peoples—in harmony, together. Pigmentation differences have no place. . . . As in genuine democracy, only performance counts." His musicians also knew they could count on Granz should any dicey situations ever arise. He traveled with the group and was very clear every step of the way how he expected his troupe to be treated: fairly—on airplanes, in hotels, in restaurants. White drummer Stan Levey remembered, "We'd all show up in the lobby and [there'd be] a lot of, you know, throat-clearing, and he'd say, 'This is our group. Let's have our rooms.' He was terrific. Norman really broke a lot of barriers. We just showed up: 'Here we are.'"

Of course, they met with some resistance along the way. In July 1954, for example, Granz had booked Ella, Georgiana Henry, and John Lewis on a first-class Pan American Airways flight to Australia, where they would be playing some concerts. But when the plane stopped for a layover in Honolulu, Ella and her traveling companions were bumped from the flight so that white passengers could take their seats. All of Ella's Sydney bookings had to be canceled. Granz was furious and sued the airline. His statement read, "The refusal was willful and malicious and was motivated by prejudice . . . because of their race and color, and this conduct subjected the plaintiffs to unjust discrimination and undue and unreasonable prejudice." Adding insult to injury, the airline hadn't even let them retrieve their belongings from the plane before it took off without them. The case was settled out of court, but it was not reported if Ella and her group received any money for their losses.

Some disgruntled club owners who didn't like Granz's position on things took issue with him. During the 1955 fall JATP tour, Ella and the troupe were in Texas, where it seemed the local Houston police had their noses out of joint about the integrated performance, and they decided to take their frustration out on Granz's folks. Five policemen made their way into Ella's dressing room, intent on causing trouble. They found Dizzy Gillespie and Illinois Jacquet playing a game of dice. Ella was eating a piece of pie. Granz and Georgiana were there, too. Granz was suspicious and followed one of the policemen toward the bathroom, just in time to prevent the officer from planting drugs in the band's room.

Even so, they were taken to the police station on a trumped-up charge of participating in an illegal dice game, and the matter had to be dealt with. "They took us down[town]," Ella remembered, "and then when we got there, they had the nerve to ask for an autograph." All charges were eventually dropped, and it seemed clear to the press that it was a case of police harassment. And according to at least one biographer, Geoffrey Mark Fidelman, the incident was resolved between the first and second performances of the night, so the show still went on.

Another incident involved a hotel in Ohio that would not let Granz's band members room with each other unless they were the same color. Granz reported the hotel to the NAACP and made headlines.

Fighting racism wasn't the only thing for which Granz worked tirelessly. From the beginning of his relationship with Ella, he had wanted to get her contract away from her manager Moe Gale and sign her up both under his management and to his record label. Gale was wary of Granz's new venture, as he was a one-man operation at the time, and Decca had sophisticated distribution processes in place for their records. Gale wasn't sure Granz's label would be around for the long haul. But Granz wasn't going anywhere.

In 1949, Ella had one year left on her contract with Decca. Granz wanted her, but so did Gale. After all, she had come in second in *Metronome*'s first All Time All Star Poll (Billie Holiday came in first). Granz offered Milt Gabler at Decca $25,000 for her contract. Gabler replied, "Norman, I love Ella just as much as you do, and I wouldn't sell her contract for any money in the world." In fact, Ella had signed with Gale when she was quite young and naïve and had given him her power of attorney, which meant that legally Gale could make decisions and act on Ella's behalf. Gale used that power to commit Ella to three more years at Decca.

Granz was not happy. Although Gale had been in charge of booking her gigs, it was Granz who was shaping her career and helping her become the star she was destined to be. His hands tied for the time being, Granz took the opportunities he could to tell the press that Decca wasn't giving Ella good enough material and wasn't showcasing her to her potential. The critics' opinions, however, varied on this subject.

Amazingly, no matter how popular and skilled Ella ever became, she retained a piece of self-doubt and had anxiety over most performances. Granz said, "I have yet to see her do a show when she wasn't nervous. We can be at an afternoon concert playing to a small house in Mannheim, Germany, in the fifth week of a tour, doing the same show she's done every day, and she'll come backstage afterward and say, 'Do you think I did all right? I was so scared out there!'" Perhaps it was the fact that music had gotten her out of a life on the streets that made her nervous about slipping up. A fellow musician said, "Whenever she hears a crowd mumbling she feels that they are discussing her—and always unfavorably. I think she lays so much stress on being accepted in music because this is the one area of life into which she feels she can fit successfully. . . . She wants desperately to be accepted."

Ella was well aware of her fears: "I'm just trying to be myself out there and get over some of that self-consciousness I have." Pianist Paul Smith played with Ella at the fancy Fairmont Hotel in San Francisco. He said, "She broke all records there. Yet every time we went there, she'd still look around the curtain and say, 'I hope they like me.' I'd say, 'How can they *not* like you!'"

Even in her later years, Ella was concerned with what people thought of her. Janis Siegel is one of the four singers that make up the Manhattan Transfer, a vocal group known for their stellar sound that encompasses jazz, pop, and big-band styles. Siegel had the occasion to present at the Grammy Awards with Ella. About the rehearsal session, Siegel said, "We did a version of 'How High the Moon' together. . . . She scats and then looks at us and says, 'Was that all right?' It was like God looking at us and saying I just created the Grand Canyon. Is it okay?" Her response could also be interpreted as having a sense of security about her, as well. She knew who she was, and wasn't afraid to invite input from others around her. She often interacted with audiences, talking to them and laughing. She was always looking to please the people. Siegel said, "One's idols are often disappointing when met, but . . . [I] found a warm, wonderful and unpretentious lady. She was oblivious to my rapturous stares. . . . Instead she sang . . . and invited us all over for coffee. My admiration for her increased ten-fold that day. When I think of a standard of excellence as a singer, I always think of Ella."

Ella's mix of security and self-doubt continued throughout her career. Musician John Chilton relayed a story about playing with Ella and witnessing her preparations before going onstage. It was understood by her bandmates that she should be left alone during this time. "It was a four-night season. . . . I was there every evening. . . . I've talked about this subsequently to other musicians who have worked with her, and they say it's been much the same with Ella for decades. . . . A few minutes before she went on, she would go to the same spot on the side of the stage, and she seemed to go through a series of movements, a pattern of behavior where she was literally psyching herself up to go onstage. No one went within yards of her because this was a definite ritual." But onstage, the love of singing and the adrenaline of performing took over, transforming her back into a woman confident in herself.

While other musicians often turned to drugs or alcohol as a means of coping with stress, Ella may have used food. She ate well, and often. She enjoyed cooking and sharing meals with friends. Her weight troubled her, though, and fluctuated most of her life as she went on and off diets. In 1964, *Time* magazine ran a nice, but unattributed, piece on Ella, and included an anecdote about her weight. "She is supersensitive about her weight, and understandably cried through the night once when—after she had performed with another heavy singer—a critic wrote: 'Last night the stage contained 600 lbs. of pure talent.'" And Ella once said, "I look at myself and I say, 'Now, Ella, you could lose that weight and you could be just like so and so.' . . . And then . . . I'll just feel sorry for myself, which is wrong."

There was a sweetness that accompanied Ella's self-consciousness, a sweetness that made people close to Ella feel very protective of her—including her press agents. She didn't like interviews, and they were kept brief and general whenever possible. With a few close friends, she opened up, but it didn't seem to be in her nature to do so completely. There is no doubt that singer Mel Tormé was a trusted friend of Ella's and still he said, "I adore Ella. Every time we see each other there's a lot of hugging and kissing, and she's come to see me several times. . . . But I don't really *know* her very well." And when it came to business, she certainly preferred having it handled for her. That is why Moe Gale had so much control over her early career. She trusted him to handle her business affairs, and that was that. Her desire was to focus on the singing.

In 1950, Milt Gabler arranged for Ella to make a record for Decca called *Ella Sings Gershwin*. Songs such as

"Someone to Watch Over Me" and "I've Got a Crush on You" highlighted her voice beautifully. She had a way of singing the Gershwin songs much the same way Fred Astaire sang them—as they were written, straightforward and clear. This was something George and Ira Gershwin greatly appreciated. Ella's soulful voice had the power to make the music the best it could be. It was the *Ella Sings Gershwin* album that gave Granz the idea to do his songbook series. Ira Gershwin helped out personally on Ella's future recording of *Ella Fitzgerald Sings the George and Ira Gershwin Songbook* and later said, "I never knew how good our songs were until I heard Ella Fitzgerald sing them."

In 1951, Ray and Ella moved to Queens, New York. Ella was not able to have children, and the couple had adopted Ella's nephew from Ella's half-sister Frances in 1948. Frances was not able to care for her son and she and Ella were very close, so the family found a solution together. Ella and Ray named him Ray Jr., and the same woman who had cared for Ella as a young girl—her aunt Virginia—helped look after him. The move to Queens gave the couple more room for their family.

In the meantime, Ray Sr.'s career was also going extremely well, and he was spending more and more time on the road with Oscar Peterson's band. In March 1952, Ella went back on tour with Granz's JATP on its first European tour. She followed this with a stateside run in September and October, and Decca made sure she had new recordings out in time to help promote them. When Ella's contract with Moe Gale came to an end in 1953, Granz and Ella finally made it official—he took over as her manager. Unfortunately, during the financial transfer, it was discovered that Gale had not been managing Ella's money well and had neglected to put aside money to pay taxes. As a result, Ella owed a large debt to the government. Perhaps to prove his dedication to Ella and her career, Granz paid off the debt with his own money. Ella would never forget that loyalty.

But while Ella's relationship with Granz was growing, the stresses of keeping up with two busy careers took a heavy toll on Ella and Ray's marriage. Although they had chances to spend time together when he was backing her with his trio or when she was touring with JATP, their separate careers also forced them apart.

The couple divorced in August 1953, and Ella retained custody of Ray Jr. Decades later, in a radio program called "Ella by Daylight," produced by Manhattan Transfer singer Janis Siegel in 1996, Ray Brown looked back on their breakup and said, simply, "If it's meant to be I guess it will stay, if it isn't, I don't care what you do, it probably won't work."

Early in 1954, Ella had her first medical scare. She had a node on her throat—a potentially devastating complication for a singer, which can damage a voice—and was rushed to the hospital to have it surgically removed. She was the perfect patient, and she took care not to speak much for six weeks, in order to let her throat heal properly. She made a full recovery, and by March was back in the recording studio.

And in June, Ella celebrated nineteen years in the business at a star-studded party at the Basin Street East nightclub in Manhattan. Famous singers such as Harry Belafonte, Pearl Bailey, and Eartha Kitt performed in her honor. Ella was given a plaque from Decca Records to mark twenty-two million records sold. This would be a huge achievement today—at the time it was extraordinary.

One of the greatest things about Ella—always—was her enthusiasm. She looked on the bright side and took joy in her work. Making others happy made her happy. "I guess what everyone wants more than anything else in the world is to be loved. And to know that you people love me and my singing is too much for me. Forgive me if I don't have all the words. Maybe I can sing it and you'll understand." Ella was never afraid to honestly express herself, and it endeared her to the world.

The following month Ella appeared at the first Newport Jazz Festival. The upper-class white setting of Newport, Rhode Island, was a long way from jazz's roots. But in 1954, a Newport couple who loved the music invited jazz lover and promoter George Wein to help them put together a jazz festival. He said, "I felt that jazz could use a coming together. . . . Jazz musicians needed a festival. By bringing many groups together we could draw many kinds of jazz fans." And they did. The Newport Jazz Festival quickly became internationally known.

The next year, 1955, brought Ella to the large and small screen. On television, she made a guest appearance in December on Tennessee Ernie Ford's popular variety show on NBC. That same month, she also guest-starred—along with Nat King Cole, comedian Red Skelton, and actress Debbie Reynolds—on the CBS variety show *Ford Star Jubilee*. Ella's second feature-film appearance was for the movie *Pete Kelly's Blues*, starring Jack Webb. She played a nightclub singer named Maggie Jackson and sang three songs: "Hard Hearted Hannah," "Ella Hums the Blues," and the title song, "Pete Kelly's Blues." The movie was based on a radio series, in which the role of Maggie had been performed by a white singer. The film also featured singer Peggy Lee, who was nominated for an Oscar for her performance. These TV and movie opportunities continued to expand Ella's exposure, giving more of the mainstream public—not just jazz enthusiasts—the chance to love her, too.

Eight

"She was like a fairy godmother to all children."

IN 1955, GRANZ started a new record label just for Ella called Verve. Soon, other artists were signed, too. It quickly became the top of the top for jazz, and still exists today, recording such jazz greats as Diana Krall and Natalie Cole. Granz eventually worked out a deal with Milt Gabler at Decca Records to release Ella from her contract. In exchange, he gave permission for Decca to make a record with some other artists that Granz represented.

Now that Ella was free to record for Verve, Granz wanted her to record the major American songwriters. He came up with a plan for her to do a series of songbooks covering such American icons as Cole Porter,

Ella with Dizzy Gillespie (top), Illinois Jacquet (second from top), and other musicians. She spent most of her time touring all over the world.

Jerome Kern, and Irving Berlin. Granz had thought his idea through carefully. He said, "I was interested in how I could enhance Ella's position, to make her a singer with more than just a cult following amongst jazz fans." At the outset, Ella was skeptical. "First I thought . . . what is Norman doing . . . who wants to listen to me singing this. But it was funny, I just gained oh so many fans all over the world. So, it was like a new beginning."

On February 7, 1956, Ella stepped into the studio to record what would be her first release with Verve: *Ella Fitzgerald Sings the Cole Porter Songbook,* which included hits such as "Just One of Those Things" and "Too Darn Hot." It went on to become a best-selling jazz record, but it was not necessarily the best of the series. Although Ella was known for getting things right very quickly, some of the songs sound as though they were overly rushed. A musician working on the sessions said, "We'd run down the verse, just to make sure she knew it, and bang, we'd record it!" Despite this, the reviews were wonderful.

Ella's career was going gangbusters. She appeared on many more television variety shows, such as *The*

Dinah Shore Show. On one episode, she sang alongside opera star Joan Sutherland and Dinah Shore, doing a funny rendition of Gilbert & Sullivan's "Three Little Maids." Ella went on to be a repeat guest star on *The Dinah Shore Show* for years. Pianist Lou Levy said of her, "One good thing about Ella, she could laugh at herself." Ella also sang alongside favorites such as Jimmy Durante and Mel Tormé, who loved to scat with Ella. Watching these old clips, it certainly appears that the performers are having as much fun as the audience.

But for all the fun they were having, Ella's touring schedule was grueling. "We used to be out 51 weeks a year. . . . A different city every night," Ella told André Previn. But Ella did the job she needed to do. No questions. About her work ethic, Oscar Peterson said, "She was a trooper. She would be there. Sometimes the jumps would be rough in between concerts." Lou Levy said, "She worked hard when she sang. . . . She was usually tired at the end of the night."

The same year Ella recorded the Cole Porter songbook, Granz booked Ella with Count Basie at the Waldorf-Astoria's Starlight Room. William "Count"

Basie was a bandleader and pianist. He was famous for his "jumping" beat and his ability to keep big-band music alive well after its heyday with his fantastic orchestra. Booking Ella at the Waldorf was in keeping with Granz's mission to bring jazz to a whole group of people who wouldn't normally go to jazz clubs. Ella was all for it. These were well-paying gigs in beautiful clubs. But there was some work to be done to train the audience's ear, and they didn't warm up to Ella until after her first few songs. Fairly soon, though, as one reviewer put it, "Ella got 'em. She got 'em some more with 'I Love You Porgy'—had 'em groggy with 'Angel Eyes' . . . and knocked 'em out with her final blues routine backed by Basie's band." Her success at the Waldorf allowed Granz to book her at other high-class clubs.

Ella's voice was infectious. If she was singing a happy song, it was hard not to smile. And a melancholy one could bring tears to your eyes. Oscar Peterson remembered the effect Ella's voice could have—not only on audiences but on the most experienced and talented musicians, as well. "Ella used to sing on the bus. . . . Once in a while she'd suddenly just start singing. She'd bring that bus to a standstill. And this is a bus full of pretty talented guys and they would almost be transfixed in their seats. They'd become like statues." It didn't matter if Ella was overweight and not necessarily glamorous—all that mattered was her voice. Hers was a voice that on the fast tunes could have the excitement and pizzazz of popcorn being popped and on the slow tunes remind you of butter melting in your mouth. Critic Henry Pleasants ticked off her skills: "sophisticated rhythmic sense . . . flawless intonation . . . endlessly inventive . . . versatile," and then added, "What distinguishes her . . . has to do with style and taste. . . . It is not so much what she does, or even the way she does it, as *what she does not do*. What she does not do . . . is anything wrong. . . . Everything seems to be just right. One would not want it any other way."

Granz may have counted on the fact that Ella would approach the songbooks—a new style of music for her—in a straightforward manner. It was Ella's tendency not to put herself emotionally into her songs that helped her perform such a wide variety of music and gain broad appeal. Granz later said about the songbooks, "It created a whole new public for Ella, and I think that her regular jazz-oriented following liked it as well." And while Granz had a heavy hand in choosing what songs Ella was singing, it was a collaborative effort. He said, "The routine I used with Ella was . . . I would get together a hundred songs that I thought would suit Ella . . . I would sit down with Ella, and I'd say, . . . 'Now let's go through each one.'" Of course, Ella's interpretation of those songs was entirely her own.

Ella's love for music and her desire to please the audience—especially a live one—usually came shining through in her singing. Granz recalled that the simple act of choosing how many songs to do could often get tangled up in her needing to give the audience what they wanted. If, for example, he and Ella agreed before a concert that she would do six tunes, Granz teased that she would say, "'Let's make it six.' And she'll go out there and do the six and then if the audience wants fifty she'll stay for forty-four more. It's part of her whole approach to life. She just loves to sing." And Granz was extremely talented at positioning Ella so she could sing in ways that would attract the widest audience possible. The JATP music appealed to one

Ella with Louis Armstrong (left) and Lionel Hampton.

set, the songbooks to another, and the kind of records she made with Louis Armstrong to yet another. And of course, for loyal fans, there was crossover appeal for all of it.

Ella and Louis Armstrong appeared onstage together in August 1956 at the Hollywood Bowl and were in the studio the next day making their first record together, *Ella and Louis*. Oscar Peterson was on piano, and Ella's ex-husband Ray Brown—who she maintained a friendly relationship with—played the bass. Included on this album are two Gershwin songs, "A Foggy Day" and "They Can't Take That Away from Me," as well as a fun, teasing song called "Can't We Be Friends," which Ella also performed on television with Frank Sinatra. It is a delight to listen to Ella and Armstrong joke back and forth on this song, playing with the lyrics and goofing around with each other like two little kids.

Ella and Armstrong would make two more records together, both in 1957: *Ella and Louis Again* and *Porgy and Bess*, the latter consisting of jazz vocal versions from George and Ira Gershwin's opera *Porgy and Bess*. About working with Armstrong, Ella later said, "You know, it never seemed like we were really recording because he came in like it wasn't nothing to it, just gonna have a ball. And I would always mess up 'cause I'd be so fascinated watching him and he'd be talking and crackin' and making jokes and you don't know whether you should sing or laugh." In fact, Louis and Ella shared a great love of laughter and reveled in it. They had a deep affection for each other. Armstrong later told jazz enthusiast and publicist Phoebe Jacobs that Ella's love for making people happy when she was up on that stage was what made her a star.

After *Ella and Louis*, Ella recorded the next song-book in Granz's lineup. *Billboard* magazine ranked *The Rodgers and Hart Songbook* at #11 when it came out in 1957. In January of that year, Ella was in the middle of a performance at the Paramount Theatre with Count Basie and Nat King Cole, when she was rushed to the hospital with stomach pains. She had an emergency operation on an abdominal abscess. Granz canceled the upcoming JATP European tour in March, resched-uling it for April so Ella would have time to recover. In true Ella style, she bounced back quickly, and was back to work, flying all over Europe for the tour.

To make things a bit easier on herself, Ella de-cided to leave New York and move to California to be near Granz. Being close to her manager, whose offices were in Beverly Hills, made sense. She bought a house in Los Angeles, and she and Ray Jr. left New York. (In 1966, ex-husband Ray also moved to Cali-fornia.) Ella had live-in help caring for her son since she traveled so much. About him she said, "I'd sure like to . . . spend more time with Ray, Jr. I don't think I'd ever give up the tours though. Being on the road gets rough sometimes, but I'd sure miss singing to the people."

Despite her successes, Ella was lonely. On the road nearly all the time, she missed having someone to share her life with. When she met a white Norwegian producer named Thor Larsen, she fell in love again. He was tall and handsome, and he stole Ella's heart. Because they were a biracial couple, their love affair attracted some attention. Rumors that they had gotten married circulated when Larsen sent her a telegram in which he referred to himself as her husband. But that was not the case. Ella said, "It wasn't a scandal. It was just at that time people did not accept the fact of the racial situation so it became like a little headline." They were happy together, until Larsen was arrested for stealing money from a former girlfriend. Sadly, Ella found herself alone once again.

Racial discrimination was still rearing its ugly head, and Granz remained dedicated to doing his part to snuff it out. After the JATP European tour ended, he booked

Ella as the headliner at the Copacabana nightclub in New York—a club that had only begun to let black patrons in. On June 19, 1957, she became the first black headliner to perform at the Copa. The crowd loved her, of course, which gave Granz the evidence he needed to get her—and some of his other black musicians—into the big, posh clubs of Las Vegas. Granz also put together the last regularly scheduled U.S. tour for the JATP, from which came Ella's first live album for Verve. Ella also finished recording *Ella Fitzgerald Sings the Duke Ellington Songbook* that year. There were some bumpy moments, as Ellington came unprepared, but this went on to be one of her most beloved albums. And Ellington made it up to her by composing *Portrait of Ella Fitzgerald* that same year.

In 1958, when Ella toured Europe with her trio and Oscar Peterson's trio, *Ella in Rome* was recorded. But the tape was filed away and lost until 1987, when it was released for the first time. "Just One of Those Things," a difficult song to sing, is a thrill to listen to on this recording. Ella always prided herself on her diction, which she worked hard to perfect, perhaps to compensate for her lack of education. And for this Italian audience who may not have been familiar with the wordy beginning of this song, she did a fantastic job. The lyrics include:

> It was just one of those things,
> just one of those crazy flings.
> One of those bells that now and then rings,
> just one of those things.

On this recording, you can hear that sweet and innocent quality so often talked about. In between numbers Ella thanked the audience several times, often with that aw-shucks giggle that could be so bewitching. "It's All Right with Me" also showcased her versatility, especially for any listener who compares this swinging, upbeat version to the touching duet she did with Nat King Cole, which made the song funny and bittersweet at the same time.

Ella had another chance to work with Cole when they both appeared in the movie *St. Louis Blues* in 1958. Ella played herself and sang "Beale Street Blues," while Cole had the leading role as W. C. Handy. This movie was notable for featuring black actors and musicians. In addition to Ella and Cole, the cast also included Pearl Bailey, Eartha Kitt, Cab Calloway, Mahalia Jackson, Ruby Dee, and Billy Preston.

Nineteen fifty-eight was also the year of the first-ever Grammy Awards, and Ella won two. One was for Best Vocal Performance, Female, for *Ella Fitzgerald Sings the Irving Berlin Songbook*, which had been completed in March. The other was for Best Jazz Performance, Individual, for *Ella Fitzgerald Sings the Duke Ellington Songbook*, which was released in July. In November 1958, she recorded the album *Ella Swings Lightly*, which won her another Grammy the following year.

Ella also guest-starred on Frank Sinatra's variety show in 1958. It was the first of many performances the two stars would do together. They were both naturals, and they loved to sing together. Lou Levy commented, "[Frank] loved her. I mean, he didn't volunteer these kind of remarks about everybody. But he just, when her name came up, he went into rapture. They worked pretty well together." Ella performing with a popular white heartthrob crooner like Sinatra could

have been a problem. Thankfully, it never was. She said, "I don't think anybody was thinking well I was black, he was white. I think everybody was just thinking we were just singing. And that's what made the program so beautiful. It was just two artists up there singing, having a ball."

Unfortunately, things weren't always so smooth. In November 1959, Granz had booked Ella on a television show sponsored by the Bell Telephone Company. When executives from Bell told Granz he couldn't have a white musician onstage with a black musician, Granz was outraged. He argued with them, threatening to pull Ella from the show, and they agreed to allow the white guitarist to play but said the camera would not show the white and black performers on the same screen at the same time. Granz fought back. He ran a two-page advertisement in *Variety* magazine pointing the finger at the company for its prejudiced actions.

If not in television land, at least the movie industry was improving on their inclusion of blacks. Ella was once again invited to do a feature film. In 1960, she played Flora in *Let No Man Write My Epitaph*. This

Ella and Frank Sinatra, together for one of their television specials, circa 1955.

time Ella had the chance to act as well as sing, playing a down-and-out singer-pianist and giving fans a dozen wonderful songs to hear. The *New York Times* called it an "occasionally moving but rather mild film," but added that "the movie people finally have had the good judgment to allot that great lady of song, Ella Fitzgerald, a brief acting chore. . . . And as a tired 'junkie,' act is precisely what she does. For this, hail Columbia (Pictures)."

By this time, Granz's record company was a success. He was already a wealthy man. But when MGM wanted to buy his Verve label for $2.75 million, Granz sold. Ella and Oscar Peterson were his star clients, and even though he decided to move to Switzerland and pursue other interests, it came as no surprise that Granz wanted to continue managing their two stellar careers. And manage Ella he did. Of course, opinions differ over just how much control he wielded. Granz contended that his job included looking out for her interests and protecting her—which sometimes included saying no to things and making personnel decisions—but that he and Ella discussed things together. Others thought she couldn't make any move without his approval. Lou Levy said, "He'd program everything. He'd pick the songs and give me a list." Pianist Paul Smith said, "Everything went through Norman." Nevertheless, Granz and Ella had a relationship that worked for them, and she had major star power.

If Ella was in town, going to see her was the thing to do. Singer Mel Tormé said, "They will dress to the hilt and attend Ella's opening night in this hotel or that nightclub. Not because they understand or appreciate her superlative singing . . . but because it is an 'event,' a social happening, a chance to be seen and admired by peers." In 1961, Ella was even flown back to the United States from Australia just to be able to perform for five minutes at the presidential inauguration of John F. Kennedy. That event was organized by Sinatra, who wanted a star-studded cast to appear in support of the new Democratic president.

Ella lived nearly her whole life on the road and had learned to adapt. She was raring to go and tons of fun when she was on the job, but often kept to herself once the show—or recording session—was over. Count

Basie said, "As usual, when you're working with Ella, it was more like a ball than a job." And pianist Paul Smith reflected: "That's when she comes alive, when she goes onstage. When the show was over, she usually went back to her hotel with her maid. It was kind of a lonely life." Ella spoke about this part of her personality, as well: "It's a funny thing. Around people, if I'm at a party, I'm very shy, I shy away from people, but the moment I hit that stage it's a different feeling. I get nerve from somewhere, I don't know what it is, but maybe it's because it's something I love to do." Lou Levy corroborates this: "When she would walk on that stage, she'd walk out there like Rocky [Balboa] and she'd start singing and that was it, it was her place . . . 20,000 people in the palm of her hand."

Even though her stardom had made her a multimillionaire by 1965, the price to be paid was an unrelenting touring schedule that constantly took her around the world. Ella was getting older, she was overweight, and she was tired. One night, during a performance in Munich, Germany, she nearly fell over from exhaustion. She was so worn out she canceled a few concerts in England and took time to rest. Once back in the

States, Ella and Duke Ellington cut a masterpiece of an album in November 1965 called *Ella at Duke's Place*. Her scatting was fantastic, and her ballads were beautiful. She and Ellington complemented each other well. Ella did a few more live gigs, but by December, she was feeling run-down again. She had a physical to see if she was all right, and took time to recuperate. Once she was feeling better, Granz arranged for a European tour for Ella and Duke Ellington that began in February 1966.

In July of that year, Ella made her last two records for Verve/MGM before her contract expired. *Whisper Not* was recorded in the studio, and *Ella & Duke at the Côte D'Azur* consisted of several days of live performances at a jazz festival in Nice, France, with Duke Ellington. After that, Granz was no longer in charge, having sold the record company. For the first time in her career, Ella did not have a recording contract.

But during the Nice jazz festival, tragedy struck. Ella's half-sister Frances died. Ella was filled with sorrow, and flew home for the funeral, but then had to return to fulfill her obligations. She later said about singing that very next concert, "It was hard to perform . . . but I said to myself, 'You have to go and sing for her. It's the only way you can express your feelings.'"

The loss of her sister had a profound effect on Ella. She reached out to her family members more than ever before and became much more involved in their lives. She had always remained close to Frances and had already been supporting her sister and her family financially, but now Ella wanted to strengthen those relationships. Ella told publicist Phoebe Jacobs, "I decided there are children that have to be taken care of and educated." Frances's three daughters—Karen, Janice, and Eloise—lived with Ray Jr. and Ella.

In terms of her financial generosity, Ella's friend June Norton later said, "It went way past her having just nieces and nephews. She had an aunt and she had a cousin, I guess she had many cousins, how many of them she was taking care of I don't know." Ella absolutely loved children. In 2007, Phoebe Jacobs said, "She was like a fairy godmother to all children. Her one regret about her recording career was that she never recorded an album of lullabies for children." Ella's desire to provide for the needs of children continued to grow. Her desire enveloped not only her own family but young people in general, becoming more and more an integral part of her life—and a big part of her legacy.

Nine

"We're swingin' it just for you."

THE 1960s SAW many changes in the music world. Big band and bebop were out, and rock 'n' roll was beginning to sweep the nation. The British rock band the Beatles arrived on the scene and almost instantly became the most popular music group in the world. To keep up with the rapidly evolving times, Ella peppered her concerts with a variety of popular songs.

At one concert in London, after saying, "I want to please everybody, all the music lovers," she playfully performed a few snippets of her take on what country and western sounded like, then some pop, and then some soul—all just her own riffing on the different types of music. Then she said, "That's enough of that," and eased seamlessly into a Gershwin tune.

Ella and Count Basie, during a 1979 performance in San Antonio, Texas.

Another time, she performed a big-band version of the Beatles' "Can't Buy Me Love" and nicely "made it her own," as they say in the music business. But her 1969 version of the Beatles' "Hey Jude" on *The Jimmy Durante Show* sounded out of place. The occasional scatting didn't fit the song nor did the song complement her voice.

Ella kept doing what she did best, while simultaneously trying to adapt to the world around her. She even wore a blonde wig for a while, sporting the new "mod" look for her fans. She loved to please her audiences and give them what they wanted. No matter how styles changed, though, Ella's voice was in great form and her fans were loyal.

Singer Janis Siegel explains how Ella's charisma came across in one version of "How High the Moon" that was recorded during a live performance in 1947. Ella forgot entire lines of lyrics and incorporated her impromptu changes with flair. Siegel said, "What I've always loved about Ella's scat treatment of this [song] . . . is the way she sort of manipulates the audience—but in a good way, where she says . . . 'Though the words may be wrong . . . we're singin' it 'cause you asked for it . . . so we're swingin' it just for you' . . . it kind of involves the audience, [saying] this is a special thing just for you." There were many times throughout the years when the words weren't necessarily at the tip of her tongue, but Ella never let that slow her down. She was there with a scat or on-the-spot made-up lyrics that fit the situation. The hilarious comedienne Lucille Ball appeared on *The Dinah Shore Show* with Ella in 1977 and teased her about this intermittent habit, saying, "You know, Ella, you're incredible. My daughter says every time you make a mistake, they release it as a hit song." The bottom line was that Ella's priority was to make audiences happy, and she had fun doing it. When she was on a stage singing, Ella was in her element—whether she knew all the words or not.

The awards continued to roll in for Ella. In addition to the Grammy awards she had been steadily collecting, the American Society of Composers, Authors and Publishers (ASCAP) gave Ella its first award for an artist in May 1965. In January 1967, Ella was named one of nine Women of the Year by the *Los Angeles Times*.

As successful as she was, Ella was still without a

recording label since the Verve contract had ended. But in September of 1967, Granz arranged for Ella to record with the Capitol label. Granz had thought a new artistic direction would give Ella a fresh edge during the heyday of rock 'n' roll, but her first release with Capitol was a disappointing collection of gospel numbers. No matter—she was still popular enough to go on another whirlwind European tour in 1968. It was during these years that Ella talked about how the musical tastes of her then-teenage son and niece helped her stay in touch with what young audiences liked. "I went to a Monkees concert with them and now I'm a fan. . . . My niece loves the Supremes, Martha and the Vandellas, Marvin Gaye—the whole Motown bit."

Beginning in the mid-1960s, probably around the time Ella first suffered from severe exhaustion, her health became a nagging issue. Ella had frequent headaches, her weight fluctuated up and down dramatically, and she was having trouble with her eyesight. In fact, since she continued to appear as a guest on television variety shows such as *The Danny Kaye Show*, *The Hollywood Palace*, *The Carol Burnett Show*, and *The Johnny Carson Show*, she became quite good at memorizing her lines so she would not need to read the cue cards. And her stage manager always made sure to put a bright white line of tape on the stage floor so she would be able to clearly see her mark. Ella didn't want anything to slow her down. But on *The Pat Boone Show* in 1968, she, perhaps uncharacteristically, spoke of the pressure of maintaining her reputation. "Being at the top is a strain. The first time you get hoarse or aren't up to par, you think you're slipping." Regardless of her self-doubt, Ella kept on doing what she needed to do—perform for the people.

Then, on July 6, 1971, Louis Armstrong died. Ella was grief stricken and went to the funeral to mourn her friend. True to her hardworking nature, though, she flew on to the Nice Jazz Festival on July 21. But her eye problems were worsening, and she was steadily losing weight—both symptoms of the diabetes she now knew she was suffering from and was trying to keep to herself. When her eyes began causing her too much distress, she had to cancel a few concerts and see a doctor in Paris. Upon Ella's return to the States, she needed her first eye surgery, which was done at a hospital in Boston. It would not be her last, and she would need another the following year. Ella now required thick glasses to see and began to have assistance coming on and off a stage. She needed to start working a lot less, and finally gave herself a long and much-needed break.

In the fall of 1972, Ella did a benefit concert for the Retina Foundation and decided she felt up for a big gig again. She found what she was looking for in the All-Star Swing Festival at New York City's Philharmonic Hall on October 23, 1972, which included remembering Louis Armstrong. All-Star, indeed! Count Basie, Dizzy Gillespie, Duke Ellington, Lionel Hampton, Benny Goodman, Dave Brubeck, and other major players were there. The evening was filmed and later aired on television. Ella was thrilled to be there, saying, "This is a wonderful evening for me with all the greats. Best of all, I'm the only girl!"

But Ella's health still required that she take it easy—at least by her standards. Concert dates were not as closely packed together as in the past. By 1973, Granz was back in the recording business, having set up a new label called Pablo (named after his favorite artist, Picasso). Doing more studio work helped reduce

Ella's travel schedule. In a 1974 article for the *New York Times*, Ella told journalist Ernest Dunbar, "I used to work 48 weeks a year, but now we do 36 weeks, and even that is split up frequently so that we can spend more time at home. . . . I get to spend more time watching my 13-year-old niece grow up." By this time, Ella's youngest niece was still with her in her Beverly Hills home, while Ray Jr., now twenty-five years old, had moved to Spokane, Washington.

For the Pablo label, Granz started Ella off by making a duet record with guitarist Joe Pass. The two artists would make three more records together between 1973 and 1986. Although her voice changed and weakened as she got older, the underlying spirit that defined Ella's sound was always there. Of working with her, Pass said, "I could change keys with her, anything I wanted to do. She's there, she hears it, no problem! It's like another musician. I play with her and she's sort of like a horn player." Around the time of Dunbar's *New York Times* article, jazz critic Benny Green said she was still "the best-equipped vocalist ever to grace the jazz scene, having a freakishly wide vocal range, literally perfect intonation and an acutely sensitive ear

for harmonic changes." One of Ella's other collabora-
tors, though, pianist Paul Smith, could hear the effects
of time on her voice: "If you . . . don't take it easy on
the voice, there comes a time when the vibrato begins
to go on you. You've stretched those vocal chords to a
point where you can't really control them."

Time was taking other things away, as well. Louis
was gone, and then, so was Ellington. When Duke Ellington died on May, 24, 1974, Ella was heartbroken.
Just a month earlier, *Down Beat* magazine had com-
piled seventy-fifth-birthday wishes as a special tribute for him in an article titled "Love You Madly." Of
course, Ella's sentiments were among them. She wrote,
"You are the encyclopedia of music. There is nothing
we can't learn from your genius. Soul, sensitivity, jazz,
art and love all come from you." At his funeral in New
York, Ella sang "Solitude" and "Just a Closer Walk with
Thee." Ella said, "I don't know what I was singing.
I have the feeling I was singing the wrong words
but all I knew was that from where I was standing I
could look right across at his body and I was sort of
frozen. . . . I'd known him ever since I was a girl. He
used to tell me a lot of things that made a lot of sense."

That same year, in October, a special honor was

Ella and Duke Ellington rehearse for the Ella at Duke's Place *album, in this photo taken by Norman Granz.*

bestowed upon Ella. Out of sheer admiration, the University of Maryland dedicated its brand-new performing arts center with a 1,200-seat theater to her, calling it the Ella Fitzgerald School for the Performing Arts. The following year, Ella made it to Broadway. Titled just *The Concert*, the show ran for two weeks in September 1975 and starred Ella, Frank Sinatra, and the Count Basie Orchestra in what is today the Gershwin Theater. In February 1976, she guest-starred on *The Mike Douglas Show* alongside Gene Kelly and Fred Astaire. Ella's set included a medley from the new

Broadway show *The Wiz*, an urban retelling of *The Wizard of Oz* featuring exclusively African American actors. In March, Ella was back at Avery Fisher Hall in New York's Lincoln Center and she once again graced the stage at Carnegie Hall in November.

The honors kept coming for Ella, a tribute to the impact she had made on the world. In 1976, Dartmouth College gave her an honorary doctorate degree in music (Howard and Princeton universities followed suit in later years), Los Angeles declared April 11 to be Ella Fitzgerald Day, and Ella won another Grammy for Best Jazz Vocal Performance for *Fitzgerald and Pass . . . Again.* She went on to receive Grammys in 1979, 1980, 1981, 1983, and 1990. She was one of the recipients of the Kennedy Center Honors on December 2, 1979, and sat in President Carter's box at the Kennedy Center while Count Basie, Joe Williams, and singer Peggy Lee paid tribute to her.

In 1981, she starred in an advertising campaign for Memorex, a company that made audio tapes. The spot showed Ella, live, hitting a high note and shattering a glass. This was followed by the tape recording of Ella's voice being played, and also shattering the glass. Viewers then heard the notes for a third time, followed by a tagline that became famous in American popular culture: *Is it live, or is it Memorex?* Being on a television commercial like this put Ella in front of a huge audience of people who weren't necessarily jazz or music enthusiasts, thus further increasing her fame and fortune.

Around this time, Ella stopped dabbling in the newer, popular hits and went back to singing the standards. These songs were closest to her style and her heart, and made her aging voice shine the brightest. Regardless of the effects age was having on her instrument, the character of Ella's voice was rich and lush when she sang the jazz fare on which she was raised. She also knew how to manipulate a phrase to hide any lack of control. There was a character, and in fact, a history, to her voice that carried her through and commanded the attention of her listeners. She made two more records with Count Basie before he died in 1984, and each one captured the class of both of these greats.

In 1983, Granz put together a commemorative JATP concert in Japan, marking thirty years since the first time JATP had performed in that country. Ella and Oscar Peterson were the headliners. Ella's trio at the time—bassist Keter Betts, pianist Paul Smith, and drummer Bobby Durham—were there, too, as were Harry "Sweets" Edison and Joe Pass. Historian Stuart Nicholson commented: "Even though her voice is darker, her range smaller, and her vibrato less sure, there is a defiant courage in her singing."

Her courage had grown in other ways, as well. In 1983, Joel Siegel wrote a piece that ran in the *Jazz Times* called "Ella at 65." Although Ella was still shy, Siegel talked about how her comfort level in the public spotlight had grown and that she seemed more at ease talking about herself—at least, after being given some time by the interviewer to settle in. He wrote: "As she speaks, she begins to feel more comfortable. . . . After an hour, she's laughing about learning disco dances from her nieces and nephews, and passing around color photographs of her 7-month-old grandnephew's christening."

Sadly, by this time, Ella's diabetes was worsening. She was hospitalized with respiratory problems in August 1985. Upon her release, she went right back to work, delivering memorable performances again and again, despite continued difficulty with weight loss and breathing. Ella was back in the hospital the following July while touring in upstate New York. She was released, then rehospitalized in Los Angeles in August. This time, Ella required open-heart surgery and needed a much longer rest than she had been previously willing to take. She did not return to the stage until June 1987.

Ten

"When she walks down the street, she leaves notes."

PERFORMING FOR ADORING fans was healing for Ella, but it couldn't cure what ailed her. She was back in the hospital in August 1987. This time, one of her toes needed to be amputated. (Diabetes damages blood vessels, which in turn decreases blood flow. The lower parts of the body, such as the legs or the toes, can become starved for blood, causing the cells to die.) This setback required an even longer recuperation period than earlier bouts had.

Meanwhile, she was still a legend deserving of praise—and it was still forthcoming. In a ceremony at the White House on June 18, 1987, President Ronald Reagan awarded her the National Medal of Arts,

Ella lets loose with Joe Williams during the 1990 Hearts for Ella tribute in her honor.

which is the highest award given to artists by the U.S. government. Her next stage performance did not take place until March 1988, in Palm Springs, California.

Remember that 1958 concert with Ella's trio and Oscar Peterson's in Rome, which had been recorded live and then misplaced? The release of the record *Ella in Rome* came out in 1988, at a very good time for Ella. Not only did it get rave reviews, it also lifted Ella's spirits. This healthy dose of positive publicity, when most of the current press was health-related, was a welcome change. The record was like a time capsule being opened. Here was Ella at her finest, being released fresh and new during her declining years. Of course, you could listen to any one of a dozen records from decades past that captured that earlier spark, too, but this was a brand-new record, frozen in time! It was a thrill to hear her swinging so hard, and the record-buying public agreed. Record producer Phil Schaap said, "It stayed number one for the whole summer, and I know she loved it. . . . She was 100 percent positive the record was a catalyst to the reactivation of her career at this time."

While some may have wondered why an aging

singer in declining health would continue to perform as often as she did, it was classic Ella. She was not being pushed to continue by anyone, including Norman Granz. She was driven. And while the people close to her may have been concerned for her welfare at times, they also understood that she had to follow her heart. Producer Eric Miller said, "Norman honestly tried from the early eighties on to get her to retire and he was turning down gigs and Ella called and said 'I want to work.'" June Norton explained Ella's perspective as she understood it: "As long as she could get out there and sing, she didn't care if you rolled her out in a wheelchair or propped her up, she wanted to entertain. That was where her joy was." In fact, her love of performing led to traveling that had been so intense in the early eighties that pianist Jimmy Rowles had to call it quits. "We did an awful lot of what you would call *serious* traveling. Brutal, like a one-nighter from New York to Caracas, Venezuela. A one-nighter!" Rowles worked with Ella throughout the 1980s and admired her talent greatly. On the official Ella Fitzgerald Web site, Rowles is quoted as saying, "Music comes out of her. When she walks down the street, she leaves notes."

Although performing always helped to keep her in both better health and spirits, as Ella's disease progressed, she became even more private than she had been. Her secretary handled most of her fan mail, and even close personal friends had trouble getting in touch with her at times. It seemed Ella wanted it that way, and who could blame her? Of course, she was happy to come out and enjoy the limelight when she felt up to it, and there were still many more honors in store for her to celebrate with her public. In April 1989, she was the first recipient of the Ella Award, a lifetime achievement award that was created and bestowed by the Society of Singers. On December 2, 1990, Ella also had the privilege of presenting this award to her friend and fellow singer Frank Sinatra. Even though she had been very sick, her duet with Sinatra that night brought down the house. The very next night Ella was given the George and Ira Gershwin Award.

In 1989, Ella felt well enough to go back into the recording studio again. First she participated in Quincy Jones's album *Back on the Block*. On this record, she scatted alongside contemporary artist Bobby McFerrin. The other record she made in 1989 was *All*

That Jazz. Her ex-husband Ray Brown chose the music for the album, which won a Grammy in 1990. Ella's performances on both of these albums speak to her versatility and the incredible span of her career. Here was a singer who was one of the first performers to enjoy the electric microphone when it was new, and decades later she was still going strong, singing alongside rapper Big Daddy Kane! These were Ella's last records.

By this time, Ella was only doing a few concerts a month, one of which took place in Minnesota at the Midsummer Festival on June 16, 1990. When she went onstage, she said, "I hope you won't mind if I sit down and sing. That's what happens at my age." Ella was not well enough to go on any more extensive tours. When Leonard Feather visited her at home in 1989, Ella told him she was "staying home and being bored. I miss the road. I miss going overseas." But the fact that she wasn't seen much anymore didn't alter the fact that she was beloved by all.

A concert in her honor at Avery Fisher Hall on February 12, 1990, called Hearts for Ella, may very well have been a pinnacle of joy for this First Lady of Song. A benefit for the American Heart Association, Hearts for Ella was a momentous occasion, and the focus of celebration was all Ella. The difference this time was that Ella was seated in the front row of the audience instead of being in the stage's spotlight—and happily so. The evening was hosted by violinist Itzhak Perlman and singer Lena Horne. Ella watched as old friends and colleagues such as Oscar Peterson, Joe Williams, James Moody, Harry "Sweets" Edison, Benny Carter, Hank Jones, Clark Terry, Cab Calloway, Dizzy Gillespie, Jessye Norman, the Manhattan Transfer, and Melissa Manchester saluted her in song. At the end, Ella was helped from her seat to join the party, as "the audience stood, cheered, whistled, stomped, and generally made a loving fool of itself." In 1994, Leonard Feather reminisced about Hearts for Ella in an article for the *Jazz Times*: "Ella . . . was finally brought onstage by Joe Williams and wound up trading scat-libs with Williams and Clark Terry to what I described as 'an ovation bordering on levitation.'" The following year, singer Vanessa Williams cowrote and recorded a song in Ella's honor called "Ellamental," saying, "She's always been one of my favorites. I just hope she gets a chance to hear it. It's a contemporary tribute to her done in a jazz, hip-hop type forum."

Although Ella's schedule continued to slow, the accolades did not. In fact, the awards nearly filled her house! But Ella was never the type to brag. It even seemed she never really grasped how incredible she was, as her humble nature remained a constant. On December 11, 1992, President George H. W. Bush honored her with the distinguished Presidential Medal of Freedom. That same year, Ella gave her final concert at the Michigan Music Hall. She had to be helped onstage, but her magic was intact. The celebration of Ella's seventy-fifth birthday was covered in newspapers and on TV stations all over the world, showing Ella blowing out the candles on her cake.

The following year, diabetes claimed both her legs, although the news did not become public until 1994. When asked why the information wasn't revealed at the time it occurred, Ella's spokeswoman Mary Jane Outwater said, "It was nobody's business. Somebody said something somewhere. We didn't. Before we knew it, it was in the paper." Ella was a living legend, but everyone is entitled to their privacy. By then Ella was nearly blind as well, and needed round-the-clock nursing care.

She started to spend most of her time inside her Beverly Hills home, relaxing and watching her favorite shows on television—mostly soap operas and baseball. (She was a baseball fan and had a big collection of personalized baseball jackets.) Once she stopped traveling the globe, Ella seemed to more fully discover the importance of family, spending time to reconnect with her then-grown son Ray Jr. Mary Jane Outwater said of her spirits in 1994, "I've never known anyone like her. She never gets depressed, never complains; she just accepts what happens. The chauffeur takes her out every day, sometimes with her son Raymond, and they have lunch out." And Ray Jr. said, "At dinner, we listen to records. Tommy Flanagan, who was her pianist for so many years, sent her his current CD, *Dedicated to Ella*, and she absolutely loves it. . . . We have a beautiful home . . . it's nice for her to be able to have this time."

She hadn't spent much time with her son when he was growing up. And when he got older, he left home and they lost touch for a while. But Ella rectified family relationships as best she could and nurtured her connections within her family. Ray Brown Jr. later said, "When you look at her upbringing, the things that went into her life, and what she had to go through, all I can say is that she gave to me as much as she could, and she loved me as much as she could, and I always knew, and she always knew, that no matter what, we would be there." And she was there for her family in later years. When her granddaughter Alice was born, Ella said, "We have a ten-month-old young lady in our house, who has taken over the house. I can't get back home fast enough to get to that baby." When asked how she felt about needing to stay home in her later years, Ella said, "I just want to smell the air, listen to the birds and hear Alice laugh."

Over the years, Ella helped many children's charities. She was generous with her success, and Ella's work for children was generally done without bringing attention to herself in the press. In 1977, she was instrumental in raising funds to open the Ella Fitzgerald Child Care Center, knowing how hard her early childhood was and hoping to make a difference in the lives of others. She was a frequent visitor to the center and always found time to bestow her generosity on the children there. Every year at Thanksgiving, each family would receive a turkey. For Christmas, she would visit the center and sing to the children. One year in the late 1970s Ella noticed there was no piano on the premises. Sometime in the next few days, a piano was delivered as a gift for the center! Ella also brought a musical or educational toy as a gift for each child when she visited at the holidays. And at Easter time, chocolate bunnies from Ella would arrive. These traditions all continue in her name to this day.

In 1993, Ella established the Ella Fitzgerald Charitable Foundation. This active foundation gives grants that focus on child care and education issues, diabetes, and music education, as well as helping to provide food, shelter, and counseling to people in need. June Norton said of Ella's work with children, "I saw so many schools and young kids where she would give them huge grants so the little kids would have a place to go during the day when they should be taken care of. She loved children so much . . . like the Pied Piper." Fran Morris Rosman, the executive director of the foundation, lovingly nicknames the grants they give "fairy godmother grants," in keeping with Ella's giving spirit when she was alive.

Ella Fitzgerald died peacefully in her home on June 15, 1996. Her son Ray arranged a funeral at the house, and Ella's family and friends went to pay their respects. Phoebe Jacobs took a moment's solace in the idea that Ella would have been tickled that her passing had caused so much attention. Jacobs said, "I was in the family car. . . . Everybody was kind of weepy. And I said, 'Well one thing I want to tell you. If Ella was here right now she'd love the whole idea. She loved to stop traffic. . . . If she got dressed up sometime . . . [she'd say] 'I stopped traffic.' . . . Can you imagine? They stopped the traffic on the freeway for the funeral procession to go through! Ella would have loved that."

Looking back on her life, Ella must have been aware of how important two men had been to her journey—Chick Webb and Norman Granz. Without Chick, it is hard to say what might have become of the young girl trying to survive on the streets with nothing to show for herself but the voice of an angel. And Norman Granz was certainly responsible for raising

Ella to the heights of international fame and fortune. Ella—with her pure, smooth tone, innate musical talent, and sheer unrelenting hard work—and Granz, with his passion for bringing jazz to the masses and stomping out discrimination along the way, were an unbeatable pair.

Although one could argue that he should have been, Granz was not a household name by any stretch of the imagination. He knew people would "see the tall old man standing next to Ella Fitzgerald, and they don't know who he is." Certainly Ella, and countless other folks in the music industry and beyond, greatly respected Granz for his efforts and accomplishments. Perhaps in time, as the world learns more about the people who did their part to battle racism, he will become better known. While Ella was alive, Granz handled everything for her—from making her a star on the stage to helping her remain as private and isolated as she wanted to be when she stepped out of the lights. Ella was a seemingly tireless workhorse for nearly six decades, but she paid a personal price for putting her career above all else.

During the course of her career, Ella made more than two hundred albums, selling over forty million copies and winning thirteen Grammy awards. After her death, many items belonging to her were auctioned off by Sotheby's, including a watch engraved to Ella from Frank Sinatra, a pendant designed by the artist Pablo Picasso and given to Ella by Picasso's wife, and a large collection of autographed cookbooks, as well as her baseball jackets. The proceeds went to a variety of performing arts, medical, and children's charities. Her estate also donated extensive sheet music, awards, sound recordings, scrapbooks, and other memorabilia—including pieces of the shattered glass from her famous Memorex commercials—to the Library of Congress and the Smithsonian Institution, where they are archived and displayed. Ella's son Ray said the donations were "a wonderful honor. . . . To see the legacy of someone who believed in hard work carry on, I hope that someone will be inspired somehow, and hopefully in a large way." Ella's charitable spirit lives on in her memory—as well as music, music, and more music. And that's not all. When she passed away, comedian Bill Cosby said, "If you listen to anything that Ella has recorded . . . you'll hear happiness. And that's a wonderful, wonderful gift to have left all of us."

Norma Miller had similar sentiments, telling

People magazine, "If Frank Sinatra was the epitome of the male American singer, then Ella was the female side." Singer Rosemary Clooney said Ella "sang every song as if it were the first time." In May 2005, Ella was posthumously given the 2005 Ford Freedom Award, which recognizes African Americans who have made lasting and positive changes to the world. Her son accepted the award in her name. And in June 2006, she was the first person to be inducted into the Apollo Legends Hall of Fame. The U.S. Postal Service honored her posthumously in January 2007 with her very own stamp. Ray Brown Jr. commented that she would be "very pleased and a little surprised." He added, "She didn't go through life expecting all the accolades that she got. She was just happy to do her thing and be the best that she could be."

Ella's legacy is still going strong. In July 2007, a collection of previously unreleased songs were issued in a new album called *Love Letters from Ella*, in time to celebrate what would have been her ninetieth birthday. By August, Billboard's 200 had *Love Letters* at #97, putting Ella back on the U.S. pop charts for the first time in thirty-eight years.

There were many written tributes paid to Ella after her death, but none more true to Ella's spirit or more appropriately titled than *New York Times* critic Margo Jefferson's piece "Ella in Wonderland." Ella was indeed our Alice—all at once simple and complex, innocent and savvy. Ella—singing her heart out, singing her whole life long, singing and spinning, as Jefferson so eloquently put it, "autobiographical straw into musical gold." A most beautiful musical tribute was paid to Ella at her funeral by Keter Betts, who played "Poor Butterfly" on his bass, offering a touching analogy between Ella's life and butterflies that play on air, pollinate flowers to make them more beautiful, and fly away. Betts said, "Butterflies are I think one of the most beautiful creations of God. . . . There are some [people] . . . that are butterflies. And they come and they pollinate people's minds, and when they go away, in the case of music you have CDs and tapes and memories of seeing them. And they fly away. . . . And at the end [of the song] . . . we hear the butterfly wings and then watch the butterfly fly away." Betts blew a kiss in the air and waved good-bye.

<h1>Source Notes</h1>

INTRODUCTION

"When you listen . . .": Gans, Charles J. "Fitzgerald & Her Fans."

"Male or female . . .": (NPR transcript)

"She was the best . . ." and "Ella was divine . . .": American Masters, "Ella Fitzgerald."

"Man, woman and child . . .": Gourse, *The Ella Fitzgerald Companion*, 114.

CHAPTER ONE

"We were *all* poor . . .": Nicholson, *Ella Fitzgerald*, 5.

"We had a little fight . . ." "Ella would always . . ." and "a very happy girl . . .": Nicholson, *Ella Fitzgerald*, 6.

"My mother had . . .": American Masters, "Ella Fitzgerald."

"She just smiled . . .": Nicholson, *Ella Fitzgerald*, 7.

"She would get . . .": Nicholson, *Ella Fitzgerald*, 6.

"When the bands got . . .": American Masters, "Ella Fitzgerald."

"She was some . . .": Fidelman, *First Lady of Song*, 6.

"Snake Hips Tucker . . ." and "There was a man . . .": American Masters, "Ella Fitzgerald."

"He made her . . .": Nicholson, *Ella Fitzgerald*, 14.

"I sensed that he . . ." "She [Ella] probably was running . . ." and "She ended up . . .": American Masters, "Ella Fitzgerald."

"She hated the place . . .": Bernstein, "Ward of the State."

"She never cried . . .": American Masters, "Ella Fitzgerald."

CHAPTER TWO

"She [stayed] with people . . .": Bernstein, "Ward of the State."

"We decided that . . .": Nicholson, *Ella Fitzgerald*, 17.

"I'm going to make . . ." and "We used to go . . .": American Masters, "Ella Fitzgerald."

"Folks hold on now. . . .": Gourse, *The Ella Fitzgerald Companion*, 114.

"And now this . . ." and "I was so surprised . . .": American Masters, "Ella Fitzgerald."

"We were opening . . ." and "of a beautiful girl . . . her name's Ella.": Nicholson, *Ella Fitzgerald*, 34.

"You're not puttin' . . ." and "If you don't listen . . .": Nicholson, *Ella Fitzgerald*, 35.

"When he brought her . . .": American Masters, "Ella Fitzgerald."

"took care of her . . .": Nicholson, *Ella Fitzgerald*, 37.

"We all kidded her. . . .": Fidelman, *First Lady of Song*, 13.

"spent most of her . . . offered her a job.": Gourse, *The Ella Fitzgerald Companion*, 18.

"She appeared one night . . .": Gourse, *The Ella Fitzgerald Companion*, 20.

CHAPTER THREE

"so knocked out . . .": Nicholson, *Ella Fitzgerald*, 37.

"Miss Fitzgerald should . . .": Nicholson, *Ella Fitzgerald*, 38.

"began to see that . . .": Nicholson, *Ella Fitzgerald*, 39.

"After we made . . .": Fidelman, *First Lady of Song*, 14.

"She knew exactly . . ." and "She could sight-read . . .": Nicholson, *Ella Fitzgerald*, 38.

"She came into . . .": Nicholson, *Ella Fitzgerald*, 41.

"at the Savoy . . .": Nicholson, *Ella Fitzgerald*, 37.

"A great band like . . .": Fidelman, *First Lady of Song*, 16.

"What a future . . .": Nicholson, *Ella Fitzgerald*, 42.

"When I first started . . .": American Masters, "Ella Fitzgerald."

"Things went so good . . .": Feather, *From Satchmo to Miles*, 90.

"I liked the song . . ." and "She's not as nice . . .": Nicholson, *Ella Fitzgerald*, 46.

"So he [Robbins] began . . .": Nicholson, *Ella Fitzgerald*, 48.

"The Webb band never . . ." and "badly written 'white' . . .": Nicholson, *Ella Fitzgerald*, 49.

"The band played . . .": Nicholson, *Ella Fitzgerald*, 50.

"We used to go . . .": Nicholson, *Ella Fitzgerald*, 55–56.

"She was always . . .": Nicholson, *Ella Fitzgerald*, 53.

"This is the turning point . . .": Fidelman, *First Lady of Song*, 20.

"Anybody that misses . . ." and "Ella Fitzgerald's singing . . .": Nicholson, *Ella Fitzgerald*, 51.

CHAPTER FOUR

"This is when that . . .": Nicholson, *Ella Fitzgerald*, 53.

"She put it on . . .": Fidelman, *First Lady of Song*, 23.

"Chick started to pack . . ." and "We broke record . . .": Nicholson, *Ella Fitzgerald*, 54.

"I'd absolutely almost . . .": American Masters, "Ella Fitzgerald."

"One time in Columbia . . .": Wyman, *Ella Fitzgerald*, 31.

"band men who . . .": Gourse, *The Ella Fitzgerald Companion*, 29.

"The guys in the band . . .": Nicholson, *Ella Fitzgerald*, 58.

"Anything happens to me . . .": Nicholson, *Ella Fitzgerald*, 61.

"It was the biggest . . .": Feather, *From Satchmo to Miles*, 91.

"He was the kind . . .": Gourse, *The Ella Fitzgerald Companion*, 27.

"Later she sent . . .": Nicholson, *Ella Fitzgerald*, 58.

"That's who she . . .": Nicholson, *Ella Fitzgerald*, 67.

"We just started . . .": Gourse, *The Ella Fitzgerald Companion*, 104.

"You just keep . . .": Fidelman, *First Lady of Song*, 26.

"She wanted somebody . . .": American Masters, "Ella Fitzgerald."

"The higher-ups . . . didn't want . . .": Nicholson, *Ella Fitzgerald*, 64.

"Look, give the guys . . .": Nicholson, *Ella Fitzgerald*, 73.

CHAPTER FIVE

"Best Ella's done . . .": Fritts and Vail, *Ella Fitzgerald*, 60.

"The driving power . . .": Fritts and Vail, *Ella Fitzgerald*, 61.

"This was a low . . .": Fidelman, *First Lady of Song*, 40.

"I never liked . . .": Nicholson, *Ella Fitzgerald*, 80.

"When I started . . .": Nicholson, *Ella Fitzgerald*, 78.

"Singers didn't make . . .": Nicholson, *Ella Fitzgerald*, 79.

"She's never done . . .": Nicholson, *Ella Fitzgerald*, 81.

"Her art was . . .": Graham, "A Woman of Nerve and Verve."

"We couldn't get . . ." "We used to take . . ." and "I worked with the band . . .": American Masters, "Ella Fitzgerald."

"isn't as easy . . .": Gourse, *The Ella Fitzgerald Companion*, 37.

"she almost had . . .": Nicholson, Ella Fitzgerald, 70.

"Somehow or other . . .": Nicholson, *Ella Fitzgerald*, 105.

"Need we draw . . .": Gourse, *The Ella Fitzgerald Companion*, 44.

"Ella had become . . ." and "Other girl singers . . .": Nicholson, *Ella Fitzgerald*, 86.

"She just kept . . .": Nicholson, *Ella Fitzgerald*, 91.

"You take these . . .": Graham, "A Woman of Nerve and Verve."

"Moe Gale continued . . .": Nicholson, *Ella Fitzgerald*, 87.

"Ella's great phrasing . . .": Fritts and Vail, *Ella Fitzgerald*, 75.

"Ella provided as many . . .": Fritts and Vail, *Ella Fitzgerald*, 76.

"I really don't know . . .": Terry, "Dizzy Gillespie."

"playing chord changes . . .": Ward and Burns, *Jazz*, 294.

"He didn't care . . .": Ward and Burns, *Jazz*, 293.

"[He] never merely . . .": Ward and Burns, *Jazz*, 320.

"My appreciation for . . ." and "I used to get thrilled . . .": Nicholson, *Ella Fitzgerald*, 96.

"Listening to Dizzy . . .": Siegel, "Ella at 65."

"With the horns . . .": American Masters, "Ella Fitzgerald."

"I think she brought . . .": Nicholson, *Ella Fitzgerald*, 92.

"Fitzgerald did what . . .": Graham, "A Woman of Nerve and Verve."

"We would go . . .": Nicholson, *Ella Fitzgerald*, 97–98.

"Do you want . . . as you can get.": Tracy, "Rhythm + Rosin = Royalty."

CHAPTER SIX

"This one pays . . ." and "'Lady Be Good' . . .": Nicholson, *Ella Fitzgerald*, 99.

"You saw right . . .": Fritts and Vail, *Ella Fitzgerald*, 83.

"'Lady Be Good' . . . represents . . .": Gourse, *The Ella Fitzgerald Companion*, 46.

"She wasn't born . . .": Gourse, *The Ella Fitzgerald Companion*, 136–37.

"Charlie got up . . ." and "He had a completely . . .": Ward and Burns, *Jazz*, 305.

"He was the other . . .": Ward and Burns, *Jazz*, 306.

"sometimes I couldn't tell . . .": Ward and Burns, *Jazz*, 320.

"The rhythmic patterns are . . .": Harman, "Gillespie Gives Concert."

"A new era of jazz . . .": Nicholson, *Ella Fitzgerald*, 102.

"Your music reflects . . .": Ward and Burns, *Jazz*, 334.

"From the first note . . .": Ward and Burns, *Jazz*, 345.

"I was in a bit . . . in New York" and "We went on tour . . .": Nicholson, *Ella Fitzgerald*, 109.

"A capacity crowd turned out . . .": Fritts and Vail, *Ella Fitzgerald*, 86.

"'I don't like to . . .": Fritts and Vail, *Ella Fitzgerald*, 91.

"In those years . . .": Nicholson, *Ella Fitzgerald*, 113.

"danced and jived . . ." and "ear-splitting ovation": Fritts and Vail, *Ella Fitzgerald*, 93.

"most uneven . . . a reflection . . .": Gourse, *The Ella Fitzgerald Companion*, 136.

"Bop is a flop—commercially": Ward and Burns, *Jazz*, 358.

"It was Decca's . . .": Gourse, *The Ella Fitzgerald Companion*, 135.

"first million-selling disc . . ." and "No jazz show . . .": Gourse, *The Ella Fitzgerald Companion*, 149.

"non-musicians who . . .": Nicholson, "Jazz: Norm's on Form."

"Black musicians were . . .": McDonough, "Norman Granz."

CHAPTER SEVEN

"Ella Fitzgerald sang . . .": Nicholson, *Ella Fitzgerald*, 119.

"He gave jazz . . . in your life.": American Masters, "Ella Fitzgerald."

"Negro music appeals . . .": Ward and Burns, *Jazz*, 392.

"Jazz is America's . . ." and "We'd all show . . .": Ward and Burns, *Jazz*, 393.

"The refusal was willful . . .": Nicholson, *Ella Fitzgerald*, 148.

"They took us down[town] . . .": Ward and Burns, *Jazz*, 393.

"Norman, I love Ella . . .": Nicholson, *Ella Fitzgerald*, 127.

"I have yet to see . . .": Feather, *From Satchmo to Miles*, 93.

"Whenever she hears . . .": Feather, *From Satchmo to Miles*, 94–95.

"I'm just trying . . .": Gourse, *The Ella Fitzgerald Companion*, 72.

"She broke all records . . .": Nicholson, *Ella Fitzgerald*, 177.

"We did a version . . ." and "One's idols are . . .": Siegel, Janis, author interview.

"It was a four-night . . .": Nicholson, *Ella Fitzgerald*, 131.

"She is supersensitive . . .": Gourse, *The Ella Fitzgerald Companion*, 77.

"I look at myself . . .": American Masters, "Ella Fitzgerald."

"I adore Ella . . . .": Nicholson, *Ella Fitzgerald*, 3.

"I never knew how good . . .": Gourse, *The Ella Fitzgerald Companion*, 119.

"If it's meant to be . . .": Siegel and Morgenstern, "Ella by Daylight."

"I guess what everyone . . .": Fidelman, *First Lady of Song*, 78–79.

"I felt that jazz . . .": Ward and Burns, *Jazz*, 388.

CHAPTER EIGHT

"I was interested in how . . .": Gourse, *The Ella Fitzgerald Companion*, 79.

"First I thought . . .": American Masters, "Ella Fitzgerald."

"We'd run down . . .": Nicholson, *Ella Fitzgerald*, 159.

"One good thing about . . ." "We used to be . . ." "She was a trooper . . ." and "She worked hard . . .": American Masters, "Ella Fitzgerald."

"Ella got 'em . . .": Nicholson, *Ella Fitzgerald*, 161.

"Ella used to sing . . .": American Masters, "Ella Fitzgerald."

"sophisticated rhythmic sense . . . any other way": Gourse, *The Ella Fitzgerald Companion*, 114.

"It created a whole new . . ." and "The routine I used . . .": Gourse, *The Ella Fitzgerald Companion*, 79.

"'Let's make it six.' . . .": Feather, *From Satchmo to Miles*, 94.

"You know, it . . .": American Masters, "Ella Fitzgerald."

"I'd sure like to . . .": Nicholson, *Ella Fitzgerald*, 169.

"It wasn't a scandal. . . ." "[Frank] loved her. . . ." and "I don't think anybody . . .": American Masters, "Ella Fitzgerald."

"occasionally moving . . . hail Columbia (Records). ": Thompson, "Epitaph is Mild Fare."

"He'd program everything. . . ." and "Everything went through Norman.": Nicholson, *Ella Fitzgerald*, 180.

"They will dress . . .": Nicholson, *Ella Fitzgerald*, 189.

"As usual, when . . ." and "That's when she . . .": Nicholson, *Ella Fitzgerald*, 200.

"It's a funny thing. . . ." and "When she would walk . . .": American Masters, "Ella Fitzgerald."

"It was hard to perform . . .": Nicholson, *Ella Fitzgerald*, 208.

"I decided there are . . ." and "It went way . . .": American Masters, "Ella Fitzgerald."

"She was like . . .": Jacobs, author interview.

CHAPTER NINE

"I want to please . . ." and "That's enough of that": American Masters, "Ella Fitzgerald."

"What I've always . . .": Siegel and Morgenstern, "Ella by Daylight."

"You know, Ella . . .": Fidelman, *First Lady of Song*, 238.

"I went to a Monkees . . .": Wilson, "Ella Changes Her Tunes." *New York Times.*

"Being at the top . . .": Fidelman, *First Lady of Song*, 190.

"This is a wonderful evening . . .": Nicholson, *Ella Fitzgerald*, 217.

"I used to work . . .": Dunbar, "Ella Still Sings."

"I could change keys . . .": Nicholson, *Ella Fitzgerald*, 218.

"the best-equipped vocalist ever . . .": Dunbar, "Ella Still Sings."

"If you . . . don't . . .": Nicholson, *Ella Fitzgerald*, 218.

"You are the encyclopedia . . .": Willard, "Love You Madly."

"I don't know what . . .": Dunbar, "Ella Still Sings."

"Even though her voice . . .": Nicholson, *Ella Fitzgerald*, 234.

"As she speaks . . .": Siegel, "Ella at 65."

CHAPTER TEN

"It stayed number one . . .": Nicholson, *Ella Fitzgerald*, 235.

"Norman honestly tried . . ." and "As long as she . . .": American Masters, "Ella Fitzgerald."

"We did an awful . . .": Nicholson, *Ella Fitzgerald*, 233.

"Music comes out of her. . . .": Official Ella Fitzgerald Web site.

"I hope you won't . . .": Anthony, "A Hot Minnesota Night, a swinging Ella."

"staying home and being . . .": Schoemer, "The Scat Lady."

"the audience stood, cheered . . .": Fidelman, *First Lady of Song*, 281–82.

"Ella . . . was finally . . .": Gourse, *The Ella Fitzgerald Companion*, 185.

"She always been . . .": "Vanessa Williams: Records New Album."

"It was nobody's business. . . .": "Fitzgerald Recuperating at Home."

"I've never known. . . ." and "At dinner . . .": Gourse, *The Ella Fitzgerald Companion*, 178–79.

"When you look . . ." and "We have a ten-month-old . . .": American Masters, "Ella Fitzgerald."

"I just want to . . .": Official Ella Fitzgerald Web site.

"I saw so many . . .": American Masters, "Ella Fitzgerald."

"fairy godmother grants . . .": Rosman, author interview.

"I was in the family . . .": American Masters, "Ella Fitzgerald."

"see the tall old . . .": Mathieson, "Norman Granz."

"a wonderful honor. . . .": "Ella Fitzgerald's Estate Makes Donations."

"If you listen . . .": Kinnon, "A Tribute: Ella."

"If Frank Sinatra was . . ." and "sang every song . . .": "The Jazz Singer."

"very pleased and . . . that she could be": Schmid, "New Stamp Honors First Lady of Song."

"autobiographical straw into musical gold": Jefferson, "Ella in Wonderland."

"Butterflies are I think . . .": American Masters, "Ella Fitzgerald."

Bibliography

American Masters and Fox Lorber Centre Stage: "Ella Fitzgerald: Something to Live For." Written and directed by Charlotte Zwerin. Produced by Karen Bernstein. Educational Broadcasting Corporation, 1999.

Anthony, Michael. "A Hot Minnesota Night, a Swinging Ella." *Star Tribune* (Minneapolis, Minn.), June 16, 1996, Metro Edition.

Balliett, Whitney. *Collected Works: A Journal of Jazz 1954–2000.* New York: St. Martin's Press, 2000.

Bernstein, Nina. "Ward of the State: The Gap in Ella Fitzgerald's Life." *New York Times*, June 23, 1996, E4.

Blackman, James. Author interview. March 6, 2007.

Dunbar, Ernest. "Ella Still Sings Just This Side of the Angels." *New York Times*, November 24, 1974.

"Ella by Daylight: In a Mellow Tone." Produced by Janis Siegel and Arianna Morgenstern. Broadcast on KCRW, Santa Monica, California, September 1996.

"Ella Fitzgerald's Estate Makes Donations to Smithsonian and the Library of Congress." *Jet*, May 19, 1997, Volume 91, Issue 26, 20–21.

Feather, Leonard. *From Satchmo to Miles*. New York: Stein and Day, 1972.

————. *The Passion for Jazz*. New York: Horizon Press, 1980.

Fidelman, Geoffrey Mark. *First Lady of Song*. New York: Birch Lane Press, 1994.

"Fitzgerald Recuperating at Home after Leg Amputation Surgery." *Jet*, May 2, 1994, Volume 85, Number 26, 35.

"Ford Freedom Award." *Jet*, July 4, 2005, Volume 108, Issue 1, 13.

Fordham, John. *Jazz Heroes*. London: Collins & Brown, Ltd., 1998.

Friedwald, Will. *Jazz Singing: America's Great Voices from Bessie Smith to Bebop and Beyond*. New York: Charles Scribner's Sons, 1990.

Fritts, Ron, and Ken Vail. *Ella Fitzgerald: The Chick Webb Years & Beyond*. Lanham, Maryland: The Scarecrow Press, 2003.

Gans, Charles J. "Fitzgerald & Her Fans: A Love of a Lifetime." *Chicago Sun-Times*, April 25, 1993.

Gilmore, Mikal. "Ella Fitzgerald." *Rolling Stone*, August 8, 1996, Issue 740, 26.

Gioia, Ted. *The History of Jazz.* New York: Oxford University Press, 1997.

Gourse, Leslie. *The Ella Fitzgerald Companion: Seven Decades of Commentary.* New York: Schirmer Books, 1998.

———. *Swingers and Crooners: The Art of Jazz Singing.* Danbury, Conn.: Franklin Watts, 1997.

Graham, Jed. "A Woman of Nerve and Verve; Will to Sing: Ella Fitzgerald's Determination Matched Her Pipes on the Power Scale." *Investor's Business Daily,* September 23, 2003.

Harman, Carter. "Gillespie Gives Concert." *New York Times,* September 30, 1947.

Haskins, James. *Black Music in America: A History Through Its People.* New York: Thomas Y. Crowell, 1987.

Jacobs, Phoebe. Author interview. March 5, 2007.

"The Jazz Singer." *People,* July 1, 1996, Volume 46, Issue 1, 42–43.

Jefferson, Margo. "Ella in Wonderland." *New York Times,* December 26, 1996.

Johnson, J. Wilfred. *Ella Fitzgerald: An Annotated Discography.* Jefferson, North Carolina: McFarland & Company, 2000.

Kinnon, Joy Bennett. "A Tribute: Ella: First Lady of Song." *Ebony,* September 1996, Volume 51, Issue 11, 68–71.

Lanier, Sharon. Author interview. March 6, 2007.

Mathieson, Kenny. "Norman Granz." *The Scotsman* (Edinburgh, Scotland), December 1, 2001, 18.

McDonough, John. "Count Basie: A Hard Look at an Old Softie." *Down Beat*, September 11, 1975, 17–18, 40.

———. "Norman Granz: JATP Pilot." *Down Beat*, October 1979, 30–32.

Nicholson, Stuart. *Ella Fitzgerald: The Complete Biography.* New York: Routledge, 2004.

Nicholson, Stuart. "Jazz: Norm's on Form." *The Observer* (London, England), January 11, 1998, 8.

"Remembering Ella Fitzgerald." June 17, 1996, Transcript from PBS/KCET interview between Jeffrey Kaye and Mel Tormé.

Rosman, Fran Morris. Author interview. March 5, 2007.

Sandora, Marisa. "S'biddable." *People*, May 26, 1997, Volume 47, Issue 20, 32.

Schmid, Randolph E. "New Stamp Honors First Lady of Song." Associated Press, January 10, 2007.

Schoemer, Karen. "The Scat Lady." *Newsweek*, June 24, 1996, Volume 127, Number 26, 80–81.

Siegel, Joel. "Ella at 65: A Lot to Be Grateful For." *Jazz Times*, November 1983.

Terkel, Studs. *Giants of Jazz.* New York: The New Press, 2002.

Terry, Clark. Edited by Lee Underwood. "Dizzy Gillespie: Blownin' with Diz, Via Mumbles." *Down Beat*, April 20, 1978, 12–14, 39.

Thompson, Howard. "Epitaph Is Mild Fare." *New York Times*, November 11, 1960.

Tracy, Jack. "Rhythm + Rosin = Royalty: Ray Brown." *Down Beat*, January 29, 1976, 12–13, 33.

Ward, Geoffrey C., and Ken Burns. *Jazz: A History of America's Music*. New York: Knopf, 2000.

"Vanessa Williams: Records New Album and Says 'These Are My Sweetest Days.'" *Jet*, January 16, 1995.

Willard, Patricia. "Love You Madly." *Down Beat*, April 25, 1974, 14–19, 41.

Wilson, John S. "A Tribute to Fitzgerald with Heart and Soul." *New York Times*, February 12, 1990.

———. "Ella Changes Her Tunes for a Swinging Generation." *New York Times*, November 12, 1967.

Wyman, Carolyn. *Ella Fitzgerald: Jazz Singer Supreme*. New York: Franklin Watts, 1993.

Index

Note: Page numbers in *italics* refer to photographs.

Photo Credits